A Field Guide to Poison Ivy, Poison Oak, and Poison Sumac

Help Us Keep This Guide Up to Date

Every effort has been made by the author and editors to make this guide as accurate and useful as possible. However, many things can change after a guide is published—science progresses, regulations change, techniques evolve, facilities come under new management, and so on.

We welcome your comments concerning your experiences with this guide and how you feel it could be improved and kept up to date. While we may not be able to respond to all comments and suggestions, we'll take them to heart, and we'll also make certain to share them with the author. Please send your comments and suggestions to the following address:

The Globe Pequot Press
Reader Response/Editorial Department
P.O. Box 480
Guilford, CT 06437

Or you may e-mail us at:
editorial@GlobePequot.com

Thanks for your input, and stay healthy!

A Field Guide to Poison Ivy, Poison Oak, and Poison Sumac

Prevention and Remedies

Third Edition

Susan Carol Hauser

Foreword by William L. Epstein, M.D.

FALCONGUIDES®

GUILFORD, CONNECTICUT
HELENA, MONTANA
AN IMPRINT OF THE GLOBE PEQUOT PRESS

FALCONGUIDES

Copyright © 1996, 2001, 2008 by Susan Carol Hauser
Previously published by The Lyons Press as *Outwitting Poison Ivy* in 2001 and *Nature's Revenge* in 1996.
Foreword copyright © 1996, 2001, 2008 by William L. Epstein, M.D.

Text design by Sheryl P. Kober
Grateful acknowledgment is made to the following for permission to reprint previously published material:
Arnoldia: Illustrations from "Poison Ivy and Its Kin," © 1975 by *Arnoldia*. Reprinted by permission of *Arnoldia*.
Clinics in Dermatology: Illustrations from "Toxicodendrons in the United States," © 1986 by *Clinics in Dermatology*. Reprinted by permission of Elsevier Science, Inc.
Rhodora: Illustrations from "The Systematics and Ecology of Poison Ivy and Poison Oak," © 1971 by *Rhodora*. Reprinted by permission of *Rhodora*.

Library of Congress Cataloging-in-Publication Data
Hauser, Susan, 1942-
  [Nature's revenge]
  A field guide to poison ivy, poison oak, and poison sumac : prevention and remedies / Susan Carol Hauser ; foreword by William L. Epstein. — 3rd ed.
    p. cm.
  "Previously published by The Lyons Press as Outwitting Poison Ivy in 2001 and Nature's Revenge in 1996." —Preface.
  Includes bibliographical references and index.
  ISBN 978-0-7627-4741-2
  1. Urushiol—Toxicology. 2. Poison ivy. 3. Poison oak. 4. Poison sumac. I. Title.
  RA1242.U78H38 2008
  615.9'52377—dc22

                                                    2007049923

Printed in the United States of America

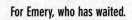

For Emery, who has waited.

Contents

Foreword

As a medical expert on poison ivy and poison oak who answers many inquiries about the subject from sufferers of this very annoying skin condition, I am delighted to be able to endorse this compact, well-written, and very informative book. The text is direct and accessible, answering a variety of questions raised to me over the years about these pesky weeds.

It is rather amazing to consider the range of misconceptions about this topic that are held not only by the public but also by many physicians. For example, a lot of people believe that poison ivy/oak/sumac leaves emanate a gas that can float over them, even if the leaves don't touch their bodies. As you will learn in this book, urushiol, the allergenic oil in poison ivy/oak/sumac, has the consistency and almost the color of 3-in-1 oil. When it is heated, it spatters like butter, rather than turning into a gas. That does not mean that downwind of a fire you will not come into contact with the oil. The spattered urushiol will land on smoke particles and can produce very serious rashes.

Urushiol also travels on the fur of pets, so this is often the source of reactions of unexplained origin. When I am told the story of someone who never leaves the house but still regularly gets poison ivy/oak/sumac, I ask a few questions that usually reveal that a pet, either a cat or a dog, goes out into the woods near poisonous plants, brings back the oil on its fur, and immediately transfers the oil to the suffering owner.

Another common mystery surrounding poison ivy/oak/sumac reactions is the change in an individual's immunity. I sometimes get a call from frantic parents who report that their twelve-year-old child has returned from camp with a horrendous bout of poison ivy/oak/sumac dermatitis, even though the child has attended the same camp for seven or eight years without any problems. It is likely that the plants were there all along, but the child had not become sensitized to urushiol and will react every time he or she comes into contact with it.

It seems as though everyone is looking for a way to cure or prevent poison ivy/oak/sumac dermatitis. Many people write to me with news of their secret cure. Unfortunately most of these lay concoctions are useless and appear to work in only a minority of people, probably through the placebo effect. One common misconception is that you can become immune to poison ivy/oak/sumac by drinking the milk of goats that have fed on the plant. As you read through *A Field Guide to Poison Ivy, Poison Oak, and Poison Sumac,* you will learn, among myriad other things, that goats do not exude the active antigen in their milk, and there is no evidence to support the notion that the milk prevents a reaction to these poisonous plants.

Much also has been said about the plants that grow around poison ivy and poison oak, suggesting they contain something that helps make you immune. The list of so-called cures is endless, and, suffice it to say, not a single one of those tested has proven to have any preventive value. In fact even the medically accepted treatment of poison ivy/oak/sumac dermatitis is not very satisfactory. In this book you will discover that over-the-counter treatments are far from acceptable, and the only thing that really works is high doses of systemic corticosteroids, used by dermatologists to treat people who are very sensitive and have explosive bouts of the dermatitis.

Control through prevention is a relatively new area of research, which has been initiated mostly at the behest of the USDA Forest Service. When firefighters come to fight forest fires in California, Oregon, and southern Washington, about one-third of them must leave the fire line because of poison oak dermatitis. We who have looked into this problem have tried to find methods to protect those who are moderately sensitive. Information on how to do this can be found in this book.

So what of the future? Several years ago the Food and Drug Administration decreed that all poison ivy/oak/ sumac antigens, used for "allergy shots," be removed from the market because the suppliers had not fully complied with regulations. At present several companies are working to meet these standards. Other molecular biologists are attacking the problem by developing "vaccines" that would block the T-cell's poison ivy/oak/sumac receptors in sensitive people, in effect knocking out the T-cell's ability to recognize urushiol when it is present in skin. This sounds like science fiction but probably is doable; and perhaps in the near future, we will see molecules available for human use that will be able to prevent people from getting these rashes.

All the currently available information on poison ivy/ oak/sumac—both scientific and practical—is in this book. It gives me great pleasure to know than an authoritative, easy-to-read guide is available for all. The book should be read through at least once and then consulted for specifics as issues come up.

> William L. Epstein, M.D.
> Professor of Dermatology
> University of California, San Francisco
> August 2, 1995

Preface to the Field Guide Edition

This book was first published in 1996. Its title then was *Nature's Revenge*. After several printings it was changed to *Outwitting Poison Ivy*, to put it on the shelf with other Lyons Press *Outwitting* books. Now it has a third life as a field guide, for that is how the book is most often used.

Not much has happened in the world of poison ivy, poison oak, and poison sumac in the last ten years. Eighty-five percent of the population is still allergic to it; the itch is still infuriating; prevention remains the best medicine, including the prophylactic washing of exposed skin with rubbing alcohol (see chapter 4). Treatment has not changed: home and over-the-counter remedies for mild cases, prescription corticosteroids for serious cases. The criteria for seeking medical help remain the same: rash on the face or over large areas of the body; rash on sensitive areas, such as the genitals; and inhalation of smoke from burning poison ivy or oak.

The good news is also the same: The rash caused by the oil urushiol is not fatal and is usually not disfiguring. Even inhalation of urushiol-laden smoke can be successfully treated with immediate medical attention if there are no related preexisting conditions.

In May 2006, poison ivy made headlines, perhaps for the first time. A six-year field study[*] indicates that poison ivy loves global warming. In an environment with such high levels of carbon dioxide, it grows larger and more densely,

---

[*] Jacqueline E. Mohan, Lewis H. Ziska, William H. Schlesinger, Richard B. Thomas, Richard C. Sicher, Kate George, and James S. Clark, "Biomass and toxicity responses of poison ivy (*Toxicodendron radicans*) to elevated atmospheric CO 2," *Proceedings of the National Academy of Sciences of the United States of America* (PNAS), May 2006, 103, 9086–9089. The article is available online at www.pnas.org. The study was conducted at the Duke University Free-Air CO_2 Enrichment (FACE) experiment.

impinging on other plant populations. In addition, the urushiol it produces is more virulent than that currently produced by plants in our forests and backyards.

Even with that news, the instructions do not change: Learn to identify poison ivy, oak, and sumac; learn how to prevent a rash even after exposure; learn how to treat a rash once it has occurred. All of this information is in this book. I hope it will help you to enjoy, without penalty, our wondrous outside world.

Susan Carol Hauser
March 2008

Acknowledgments

One of the pleasures of writing this book was listening to the passionate telling of poison ivy and poison oak stories. My thanks to family, friends, and acquaintances who shared their experiences, and to the many readers of the *New York Times Book Review* who answered my author's query.

My thanks also to Helen Bonner, Ph.D.; Marshall Muirhead, D.D.S.; Dave Carlson; Maggie Carlson; Fred Forseman; and Ginnie Forseman for reading and commenting on the manuscript. Thanks also to Wallace Wanek, Ph.D., Bemidji State University, Minnesota; Mahmoud A. ElSohly, Ph.D., University of Mississippi; Clark Montgomery, Minnesota Extension Office; and staff members at the Food and Drug Administration, the University of Minnesota, and the USDA Forest Service for patiently answering my many questions.

My deep appreciation to John D. Mitchell, Ph.D., New York Botanical Garden, for explaining to me the finer details of *Toxicodendron* and for reading the manuscript, and to Cathy Paris and David Barrington for entrusting me with a rare copy of *Rhodora*.

My debt of gratitude to William L. Epstein, M.D., professor of dermatology, Dermatology Research, University of California, San Francisco, for granting me frequent and frequently long interviews, for permission to incorporate some of his research findings into this book, and for reading the manuscript for accuracy.

These kind persons are responsible for many of the scientific and savory details herein. Errors and omissions are my own.

Introduction

"There's poison ivy down there," said my friend when I offered to trim the staghorn sumac that was beginning to block her view of the lake from the kitchen window. "That's all right, I'm not allergic," I replied. "Besides, my legs and arms are covered, and I'll wear gloves." She brought me the pruner and watched from the safety of the ridge while I let myself down onto the steep, brushy hill and scootched around on my backside, using the pruner to nip off the offending branches.

It was mid-October in northern Minnesota. The fallen leaves were pretty much melted into the ground, and I did not pay attention to the stubby little twigs and clusters of white berries that I crushed as I moved. When I was done, I was pleased with myself. I like working outside. My friend and I went into her house for tea, and I let the memory of my good deed take its place in the catalog of fall tasks accomplished.

It was nearly a week before I thought about it again. I had put on the same jeans every day, my favorites for end-of-the-summer, outdoor grubby tasks. One morning the backs of my legs began to itch, from my panty line to my knees. By evening they were aflame, and within two days they looked like I had raked them with a wire brush. I washed my jeans, but it was too late. I had poison ivy.

It is fairly unusual to reach middle age in the woods of northern Minnesota and not have fallen victim to nature's most common revenge. When I started asking friends for advice on treatment, they were surprised, knowing my foraging habits, that I had been spared to this point. And I was surprised at the pleasure they seemed to take from my plight. My previous immunity was somehow a personal affront to each of them, and they thought it served me right to finally join them in the ranks of the stricken.

As my affliction progressed, I began to understand their passion. The itching got worse, and no treatment worked for long. Fortunately there was an unending list of home remedies to try. They kept me occupied and offered new hope when I thought the only appropriate response was to fillet the backsides of my legs. I applied creams, both commercial and homemade, alternating them with astringents such as rubbing alcohol. At the end of three weeks, the original allergy had pretty much worked itself out, but my skin continued to scream, in part from the onslaught of "healing" potions that I had subjected it to, and in part from reexposure. In the several days before I washed my jeans, I had sat in them on every chair in the house. After that, whenever I sat down with bare legs, I sat on a little bit of poison ivy oil. It was a full six weeks before the adventure whimpered to a close.

When I was finally able to think about something other than skin, I attacked the subject with my usual weapon of choice: research. Again I was met with unexpected passion. Most writers on the topic seem to be motivated, as I am, by the desire to drive a spear into the heart of the monster. While it is not likely that we will ever be rid of poison ivy and its equally hostile relations, our current knowledge of the offending oil urushiol does make it possible for us to negotiate a truce with this cantankerous weed. The information in this book should help you to prevent exposure or reaction. Failing that, there is hope in the form of reasonable and effective treatment, and that information is here, too. My best advice: Learn to recognize the plants; treat your skin kindly; and do not hesitate to seek medical attention. In addition, do not assume that you are among the chosen immune. Such hubris can come back to bite you in inconvenient places.

Chapter 1
The Toxic Trio

Nature's hostility to human interference is usually manifest on a large scale, in such phenomena as global warming and ozone-layer deterioration. These retributions affect all living things. But the revenge wrought by poison ivy, poison oak, and poison sumac is reserved exclusively for the human inhabitants of planet Earth. Bears, birds, and other wild creatures eat the berries and sleep among the leaves with no ill effects.

The most common ill effect suffered by humans is a dermatitis caused by contact with the plants' oils. Rashes and blisters erupt on the skin, sometimes oozing and weeping, and always causing a pernicious itch. Less common and more dangerous is contact with the smoke of burning poison ivy, oak, or sumac plants or their parts. The oil that causes the allergic reaction is carried in smoke and can land on skin and in eyes and ears and can even be inhaled, causing serious lung problems.

In North America, poison ivy and poison oak grow happily from Mexico to Nova Scotia, except in the desert areas of the southwestern United States. Their growth requirements are simple. They prefer an elevation under 4,000 feet. They prefer sunshine but will do without. They favor drier soils but tolerate moisture. They love ground that has been disturbed and multiply freely on road embankments and along forest trails. They spread happily in city parks, such as Central Park in New York City, and in suburban backyards.

Although poison ivy, oak, and sumac are essentially the same plant, poison ivy resides in the eastern, midwestern,

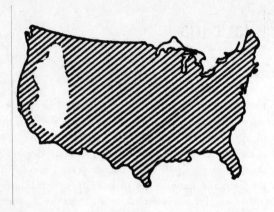

Toxicodendron distribution in the United States. It is not indigenous to Alaska or Hawaii but extends north into Canada and south into Mexico.

and northwestern United States, north into Canada, and south into Mexico. Poison oak prefers the East and West Coasts and some south-central areas of the United States. Aside from geography, the primary difference between the oaks and ivies is the shape of the leaflets.

Poison sumac, the largest of the three, contains the same allergen as poison oak and ivy and causes the same reaction. But sumac is particular about its habitat. It resides in swamps from Maine to Florida, west to the Mississippi River, and occasionally north to eastern Canada. Because of its reclusive nature, it is not much of a pest.

Actually none of the three would be a threat if it were possible to avoid exposure to them. This proves, however, to be nigh unto impossible for anyone who likes to be out in nature. Poison ivy and oak are especially ubiquitous, and sneaky. They grow as small shrubs, as tall shrubs, and as long vines that creep along the forest floor or up into the treetops.

The most common advice for avoiding poison ivy and oak is the old saw, "Leaves of three, let it be." Strict application of this rule may be appropriate for the occasional woods wanderer who is willing to remain on a beaten path. But for the nature lover who wants to get up close and friendly with local fauna, it is far too restrictive: Many benign forest plants have three leaves, or three leaflets.

As with most easy advice, in the end even the more specific "leaflets three, let it be" not only encourages excessive precaution, it does not render absolute protection. Both poison oak and ivy have compound leaves that are usually arranged in three leaflets, but they may have up to eleven leaflets.

The person who wants to be spared two weeks of scratching as payment for a weekend in the country should not only count leaflets but also learn to recognize leaf and plant shapes. In its usual perverse way, nature does not make this easy. Poison ivy leaflets are usually oval and lightly toothed. Poison oak leaflets are usually slightly lobed, like oak tree leaves. Where their ranges overlap—in the Midwest, for example—the oaks and ivies hybridize, and newcomers may be classified as both. In addition, offspring from root stalks reproduce true to their source, but those from seed may go their own way. As of 1986, according to an article in *Clinics in Dermatology*, the poison ivy species known as *Toxicodendron radicans* had nine identified subspecies (sometimes called varieties or cultivars).

Fortunately whatever the intricacies of their shapes, the oaks and ivies are predictably similar in other important ways. The leaflets of both plants are usually about four inches long. Their stems are woody. Climbing varieties have visible aerial roots. The leaflets are usually shiny—sometimes described as waxy—although they may also be dull or hairy, especially underneath. They start out a bright green and toward late summer and fall turn yellowish or reddish, then bright red.

When in bloom or gone to seed, poison oak and ivy are easier to distinguish from other plants. Variations in

Poison ivy, *Toxicodendron radicans* Shrub or climbing vine. Shape of leaflet varies; occasionally has one lobe. Usually three leaflets to a leaf, but may have more. Berries are smooth and green at first, then whitish and usually hairy. Stems are sometimes hairy. Aerial rootlets. Illustration by Vivienne Morgan.

Also extends south into Mexico. USDA, NRCS. 2007.

Rydberg's poison ivy, *Toxicodendron rydbergii*. Low, non-vining shrub. Leaflet shape may vary, but is rarely lobed. Usually three leaflets to a leaf, but can have more. Leaflets may be hairy on their undersides. Berries are smooth and green at first, then smooth and whitish. Illustration by Vivienne Morgan.

Also extends north into Canada. USDA, NRCS. 2007.

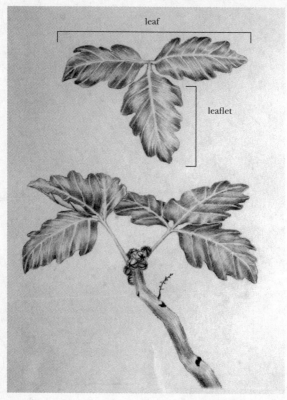

Eastern poison oak, *Toxicodendron pubescens*. Non-vining shrub. Leaflet shape highly variable from lobed to unlobed, but often resembles white oak. Usually three leaflets to a leaf, but can have more. Stems and leaves have fine hairs. Berries are smooth and green at first, then hairy and whitish. Illustration by Vivienne Morgan.

USDA, NRCS. 2007.

USDA, NRCS. 2007.

Western poison oak, *Toxico-dendron diversilobum*. Shrub or climbing vine. Leaflet shape varies from lobed to unlobed but often resembles California live oak. Usually three leaflets to a leaf, but can have more. Berries are smooth and green at first, then whitish, and are usually heavy and pendant. Berries and stems are sometimes hairy. Aerial rootlets. Illustration by Vivienne Morgan.

Poison sumac, *Toxicodendron vernix.* Rangy shrub or tall tree. Leaves may have multiple leaflets, always in odd numbers. "Rabbit-ear" shaped leaflets and drooping berries, which are white. Other sumac leaves tend to be more lance shaped, and their berries are red and erect. Illustration by Vivienne Morgan.

Also extends north along the east coast into Canada. USDA, NRCS. 2007.

the flowers and berries are unusual. Blossoms appear in early summer and are greenish white or yellow, are less than one-half inch in diameter, and have five small petals. They grow in clusters on their own three- to six-inch stems. The white- or cream-colored berries that appear in early autumn are hard and smaller than peas; they hang in drooping, loose clusters among the leaves.

During the winter the berries often remain on the bare stems, where they are eaten by birds and animals or crushed under the skis and boots of winter recreationists. Plants do not produce flowers and fruit until their third year. On male plants the flowers fall away. On female plants the flowers are pollinated and become fruit. The flowers of the male plants are more fragrant than those of the female plant and often attract honeybees (Guin and Beaman). As with all parts of the plant except the flowers, pollen, and fruit pulp, the skin of the berries is toxic to humans. The offending juices, innocently carried home on clothing and equipment and later transferred to bare skin, can cause an allergic reaction even though the plant itself slumbers under a blanket of snow.

Many of the physical qualities of poison oak and ivy are shared by their cousin, poison sumac, although usually on a grander scale. Sumac's larger flowers are the

Poison ivy look-alikes. *Outing* magazine, August 1902.

same greenish white or yellow, have five petals, and hang in clusters that may be up to eight inches long. The large clumps of drooping, yellowish berries distinguish poison sumac from other sumac trees, which have red berries that stand erect.

Unlike its smaller relations, poison sumac grows as a large shrub or as a tree that has a diameter up to 6 inches and a height of 15 feet. Its bark is coarse and gray. The shiny, compound leaves may reach 15 inches or more in length. The seven to thirteen slender, oval, smooth-edged leaflets are each 3 to 4 inches long. Their color in the growing season ranges from green to reddish and usually turns to all red in the fall. Sumac is not subject to the whims of hybridization that confuse identification of poison oak and ivy.

With a little determination hikers, campers, and cyclists can learn to avoid poison sumac and distinguish poison oak and ivy from innocent look-alikes such as wild sarsaparilla and Virginia creeper. But the amateur botanist who is driven to neat categorization will likely be driven to distraction by efforts to call the poison three by their proper Latin binomials, the naming protocol used by scientists. Edward Frankel, Ph.D., in his book *Poison Ivy, Poison Oak, Poison Sumac* reported that students described the "nomenclatural history as 'a mess,'" and he called it a "taxonomic tennis game."

The taxonomy, or classification system, of plants and animals is based on natural relationships. As with most human systems, it has back roads, alleyways, and dead ends. Poison ivy and sumac are located in the plant kingdom (humans are in the animal kingdom), in the division Spermatophyte (seed bearing). The class is Dicotyledoneae (having two cotyledons, or seed leaves). After that, the grouping gets trickier. A common feature of its order, Sapindales, is compound or cleft leaves in combination with other features such as syncarpous ovary (having two or more pistils growing together). The family is Anacardiaceae, also called the cashew family. Many members of this set share the *Toxicodendron* trait of a five-part flower with a three-part style.

Poison oak, ivy, and sumac have been in the Anacardiaceae family for as long as anyone cares to remember. Their Anacardiaceae cousins include the mango and India ink trees. These trees do not contain the oil that causes poison ivy, oak, and sumac dermatitis. However they do contain similar oils that can cause a rash similar to the poison ivy, oak, and sumac rash.

Two steps are left in the hierarchy of scientific nomenclature genus and species. It is in assigning these names that most of the confusion takes place. "There are the lumpers and the splitters," says Wallace Wanek, Ph.D., professor of biology at Bemidji State University in Minnesota. The lumpers like to classify into broad categories. The splitters like to separate according to finer details. With the capability to evaluate plants at the cellular level increasing, says Wanek, the splitters are in the lead.

Earlier in the twentieth century poison ivy, poison oak, and poison sumac were lumped into the genus *Rhus* along with plants that share some characteristics with them but do not contain urushiol, the "poison" oil that causes the contact dermatitis. Mid-century, William T. Gillis, of Michigan State University in East Lansing, undertook a major study of the trio. Following the lead of some earlier botanists, he proposed that plants containing urushiol be split off into their own genus.

Although the popular press sometimes continues to use the *Rhus* label, over the decades the scientific community has generally accepted the new genus. In fact the splitters have been so pleased with it, they continue to apply their fine-tuning to the level of species. The three common plants once known as poison ivy/*Rhus radicans,* poison oak/*Rhus toxicodendron,* and poison sumac/*Rhus vernix* now translate into five *Toxicodendron* species. The two poison ivy species are *T. radicans* and *T. rydbergii,* and the two poison oak species are *T. pubescens* and *T. diversilobum.* Poison sumac remains as one species, *T. vernix.*

This separation into species is based on detailed biological considerations. The toxic oil is identified at the molecular level, but other identifying characteristics, explains John D. Mitchell, Ph.D., of the New York Botanical Gardens, are visible. They include "lax and pendant inflorescences," meaning the flowers hang loosely down, rather than stand erect, and "a papery exocarp on the drupe," meaning the fruit has a papery skin.

Always seeking further refinements, taxonomists are probably not done renaming the toxic trio. When the plants were placed in the genus *Toxicodendron,* the two species of poison oak were named *T. toxicarium* and *T. diversilobum.* Recently the *T. toxicarium* epithet was changed to *T. pubescens* to more accurately distinguish the plant's physical features from those of *T. diversilobum. Pubescens* is a Latin word that means "hair," and, unlike *T. diversilobum, T. pubescens* has hair on its leaves, stems, and fruit.

Accuracy in the naming of plants has been an obsession of scientists since long before Carl Linnaeus, born in Sweden in 1707, introduced Latin binomials (two names, genus and species, as in *Rhus radicans*). Many of the names derive from ancient languages. In addition to *pubescens,* Latin gives us *rhus* for "sumac," *toxico* for "poison," *radicans* for "root," *vernix* for "waxy" (a quality of the "poison" oil), *venenata* for "poisonous," and *diversi* for "various." From the Greek we get *dendron* for "tree" and *lobata* or *lobum* for "lobe," describing the rounded fingers of the poison oak leaf. Some names are newer in origin. *Rydbergii* is named, said Frankel, "in honor of Per Axel Rydberg (1850–1931), an expert on western (U.S.) flora."

Shakespeare said, "A rose by any other name would smell as sweet," and poison ivy, oak, and sumac, no matter what their botanical classification or the majesty of their names, all have the power to anger human flesh and cause it to itch, it seems, clear down to bone.

The offending substance in all three is the oil urushiol (yoo-ROO-she-ol or oo-ROO-she-ol), which flows within canals in the leaves, stems and roots, and in the skin of the berries. The oil is not found, however, in the flowers, pollen, fruit (berry) pulp, or dried leaves that have fallen naturally from the plant. Apparently, as the leaves die off, the oil, along with other fluids, is drawn back into the stems. This action does not remove urushiol from leaves that have broken off from the plant, nor from the roots, nor from stems that remain standing through winter, although their urushiol can be present in less potent levels than in spring when the sap is rising.

Urushiol does no harm as long as it stays inside the structure of the plant, but it escapes with the ease of Houdini. Even the bite of an insect opens enough of a wound to release the oil. According to studies conducted by William L. Epstein, M.D., Dermatology Research, University of California, San Francisco, as little as one microgram can cause an allergic reaction in highly sensitive people. How much is that? A microgram is one millionth of a gram; a gram is equal to about two tablespoons of butter. It takes about two micrograms (two millionths of those two tablespoons) to make most people react.

The invisibility of this durable oil has led to folklore of the highest order. Attributes usually reserved for poltergeists or the "wee folk" of Ireland are assigned to poison ivy, oak, and sumac. "You don't have to touch the plant," I've been told. "You can have an allergic reaction just from walking near it."

"That's true," a friend assured me. Her daughter got poison ivy every spring from plants on a hillside across the road from their house, even though the little girl never left the yard. My uncle insisted that the rash he got around his

Flowering *Toxicodendron radicans*. A. Habit sketch. B. Female flower. C. Male flower. D. Male flower. E. Female flower. F. Ultimate branch of inflorescence. G. Longisection of female flower. H, I. Floral diagrams of alternate forms of aestivation of female flower. J, K. Floral diagrams of alternate forms of aestivation of male flowers. (Illustration by Priscilla Fawcett, Fairchild Tropical Garden illustrator retired. Reprinted by permission of Priscilla Fawcett and *Rhodora*, vol. 73, Jan.–March, 1971.)

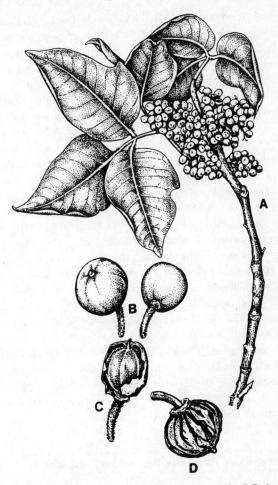

Fruiting *Toxicodendron radicans*. A. Habit sketch. B. Intact fruits. C. Fruit with portion of exocarp removed. D. Fruit with exocarp removed, showing striated endocarp, the form of the usual propagule. (Illustration by Priscilla Fawcett, Fairchild Tropical Garden illustrator retired. Reprinted by permission of Priscilla Fawcett and *Rhodora*, vol. 73, Jan.–March, 1971.)

ankles every spring had lain dormant in his flesh all year, just waiting for the season to turn so it could erupt again. And a woman I never met called in to a radio show to tell me, irrefutably, that poison ivy traveled through falling water, because she got it every time she went out in the rain.

Urushiol can, in fact, travel through the air if it is carried in the smoke or soot of burning poison oak, ivy, or sumac plants, but it has no will of its own. What it does have is the ability to retain its allergic properties even when carried on the fur of cats and dogs or transferred to inanimate objects such as clothing and tools. My friend's daughter slept with their cat, which did cross the road to the poison ivy patch. My uncle wore the same unwashed overalls every spring when he cleaned up his garden. And the woman on the radio probably picked up the same contaminated umbrella when she went out into the rain. Urushiol can lie in wait for years on the handle of a rake and still bond to human skin within five or ten minutes.

Despite our human experience with poison ivy, oak, and sumac, the *Toxicodendron* trio is not without redemption. Birds that can indulge without penalty in the berries include flickers, chickadees, and warblers. They are joined at the table by some rodents. Bees make honey from the nectar. Mule deer, horses, and cattle willingly graze the pests from human territory, as does that mammalian vacuum cleaner the goat.

Poison Ivy, Poison Oak, Poison Sumac Taxonomy

Kingdom: Plant
Division (Phylum): Spermatophyta
Class: Dicotyledoneae
Order: Sapindales
Family: Anacardiaceae
Genus: formerly *Rhus* now *Toxicodendron*
Species: (See tables)

Genus and Species Taxonomic History, and North American Distribution

Poison Ivies

Formerly one species, sometimes called *Rhus radicans,* sometimes *R.toxicodendron*[*]. Now moved to the genus *Toxicodendron* and split into two species.

Toxicodendron radicans (poison ivy); identified by ivy-shaped leaflet and as shrub or climbing vine; eastern United States, Mexico.

Toxicodendron rydbergii (Rydberg's poison ivy); identified by ivy-shaped leaflet and as dwarf shrub; central and west central United States and southern Canada.

[*]Also used for poison oak.

Poison Oaks

Formerly one species, variously called *Rhus toxicodendron*[*], *R. quercifolia, R. lobata,* or *R. diversilobum.* Now moved to the genus *Toxicodendron* and split into two species.

Toxicodendron pubescens (eastern poison oak) formerly *T. toxicarium;* identified by oak leaf–shaped leaflet and as non-climbing shrub; southeastern and south central United States.

Toxicodendron diversilobum (western poison oak); identified by oak leaf–shaped leaflet and as bush or climbing vine; west coast of the United States and British Columbia

[*]Also used for poison ivy.

Poison Sumac

Formerly *Rhus vernix, R.venenata, R.glabrum,* now moved to the genus *Toxicodendron* (still one species).

Poison Ivy

"*Rhus toxicodendron* the learned botanist calls it; and isn't that a high-sounding name for such a reprobate? Look at that aged specimen about the fence post, like a highwayman, lying in wait for the barefoot youngsters as they climb the fence to take a short cut to the swimming hole."
Outing magazine, August 1902.

Chapter 2

War Stories and Old Wives' Tales

In *The Generall Historie of Virginia, New-England, and the Summer Isles* (Bermuda), published in 1624, Captain John Smith identified a plant that was commonly called "the poysoned weed." He described it as "much in shape like our English Ivy, but being but touched causeth rednesse, itching, and lastly blisters, the which howsoever after a while passe away of themselves without further harme. . . ." Being the first person, perhaps, in the western world to describe poison ivy in writing, he was also perhaps the first to acknowledge the bum rap poison ivy gets just because it is a nuisance: ". . . yet because for the time they are somewhat painfull, it hath got it selfe an ill name, although questionlesse of no ill nature."

Before and since then poison ivy and poison oak have been subjected to pejorative names such as picry (from Greek "bitter or pungent"), mercury (a feared poison), poison creeper, and poison vine. Slander is commonplace. An article in *Country Life in America*, September 1908, reported that poison ivy "flourishes like the wicked," and the naturalist Edwin Rollin Spencer, in his classic 1940 book *All About Weeds*, referred to "this snake of the weeds" and commented that "whether it stands or crawls it is the same old Satan and should be designated as such."

Poison ivy and oak's scurrilous reputations developed in part from the dastardly itching the plants cause and in part from the perceived ability of the poison to travel through air. Efforts to debunk this myth were and still are largely unsuccessful. At least as early as August 1927, scientists tried to convince the public that "despite the

> *In the 1970s . . . I entered the Torture Ridge Run in Eugene,*
> *Oregon. . . . It was the middle of the rainy season, that is to*
> *say, the paths were horribly muddy. We ran through narrow*
> *paths with the foliage brushing up against our scantily clad*
> *bodies, and days later the nightmare began. My body was*
> *covered 100 percent from my waist to my ankles and scattered*
> *less so on the rest. . . . Poison oak had ravaged me severely*
> *and, so I was told at the (University) infirmary, most of*
> *the other race participants as well. I ignored conventional*
> *wisdom and scratched away until I was a scabbed and*
> *bloody mess. The relief from scratching and hot showers was*
> *like an orgasm, if I may, since the release from the itch was*
> *so dramatic. I remember the raised ridges running along my*
> *legs as if I had been internally invaded by some creature from*
> *a sci-fi movie. The Torture Ridge Run had truly lived up to*
> *its name.*
> —J. M.
>
> *Author's note: Very hot water can release histamines from the*
> *skin and thereby relieve itching, sometimes for many hours.*
> *Care must be taken to not burn the skin.*

mass of hearsay evidence, ivy poisoning is not borne by the air." In that month's issue of *Hygeia*, a health magazine of the American Medical Association, the story was told of a woman who had "been so careful" as to sit on a towel while eating a roadside luncheon. In spite of her efforts, she later developed poison ivy. The article pointed out that she also later wiped her hands on the towel and thereby transferred the oil urushiol, then called lobinol, to her skin.

While country goers had difficulty avoiding poison ivy and oak, the scientific community was equally frustrated in its effort to understand the nature of the poison itself.

The *Literary Digest* for July 24, 1926, reported the discovery of lobinol by Dr. James B. McNair, a scientist at the University of Chicago. Yet the same article reported the work of J. F. Couch, a chemist with the U.S. Department of Agriculture, who felt there was an additional poison component that was "volatile and capable of acting at a distance . . ." —that is, through air, without the requirement of direct contact.

Despite the gradual advance of scientific understanding of the chemical properties of poison oak and ivy, early to mid-twentieth-century prevention and treatment methods remained haphazard. McNair, in response to his own research, developed a foolproof prevention for poison oak and ivy reactions—a thorough washing with a 5 percent solution of ferric chlorid (*sic*) in a half-and-half mixture of water and alcohol. The July 24, 1926, *Literary Digest* reported that as a result of diligent use of this "'iron treatment,' ivy poisoning has become a thing unknown in the botany department at Chicago."

If the iron treatment was indeed as effective as reported in preventing reactions, it was probably due in part to conscientious washing and in part to the use of alcohol, which neutralizes urushiol (see chapter 4). Iron is not known to have any such effect.

Prior to the invention of the iron treatment, washing with the juicy stem of *Impatience capensis* or *Impatience biflora*, jewelweed, was by far the most popular response to exposure to urushiol. If jewelweed was not available, Charles Monroe Mansfield, M.D., in an article in *Country Life in America*, June 1912, recommended that the victim "take up a handful of good moist earth and rub it well into the parts." At home the favored wash was "cheap yellow laundry soap," recommended in 1924 in the *Literary Digest* and in almost every other article of the time devoted to poison ivy, oak, or sumac.

When I was about five or six, in 1937, I caught an extremely bad case of poison oak. . . . It was so bad that I was hospitalized at the Children's Hospital in San Francisco. There I was put to bed naked under a sort of cage-like structure, which held the sheets up over my body so that nothing would touch me. I was slathered in boric ointment and left to ooze for days. . . . As traumatic as it was, I have a very, very fond memory of that week as my mother sat by the bed and read what seemed to me to be all night long. We went through all the Greek and Norse myths during those long days and nights. When I was dismissed, I was told to apply boric on gauze and cover the worst patches. I believe it took about a month before I was fit to be seen in public.

—S. N. B.

If the preventive battle was lost, a victim in the nineteenth and early twentieth century did not merely give in and scratch. Remedies abounded. Many were derived from American remedies that proved their worth over centuries. The romantic rumor that American Indians were not vulnerable to urushiol is precluded by their knowledge of these treatments and by their use of poison ivy and oak as a remedy for other ailments.

The 1990 *Peterson Field Guides Eastern/Central Medicinal Plants* listed ten different herbal remedies used by American Indians to treat urushiol outbreaks. Teas, poultices, compresses, and salves were concocted from plants such as jewelweed, peppergrass, horse nettle, wild lettuce, yellow giant hyssop, lady's thumb, horse nettle, and Labrador tea, and from trees such as smooth alder, white and red oak, and beech.

The North American Indians, from Mexico up into Canada, used actual leaves of poison ivy, oak, and sumac to treat afflictions such as warts. According to William T.

Gillis in "Poison-ivy and Its Kin," *Arnoldia*, 1975, they also used the leaves to make poison potions for tipping their arrows and the supple stems to make baskets as well as spits for cooking meat. Gillis does not comment on ill effects from such use but does note that the Indians may have also used the berries in religious rituals. He reports that seeds found in a medicine man's possessions at a Mesa Verde site were "radiocarbon-dated as having grown around the 13th century." They had apparently been preserved by the dry desert air.

When the European settlers arrived, they adopted the American Indian treatments for the rash and adapted at least one of their own recipes for additional treatment. The *Peterson Field Guide* reports that poultices from the common plant bouncing bet, which grows both in Europe and in North America and was used "back home" for acne, boils, and eczema, also worked on this New World affliction.

By the turn of the twentieth century, herbal poultices and teas were giving way to more dramatic treatments. A wise country doctor quoted in the *Atlantic Monthly* in June 1923, prescribed patience as the best medicine, since ivy poisoning must, "like first love, run out its course." But to post–industrial revolution pioneers, that was inadequate advice. Innovative homegrown remedies spread with the ease of urushiol itself.

The common denominator in most new home remedies was an aggressive astringent wash. The attendant scrubbing matched the intensity of the itch better than the application of soothing lotions. The June 1923 *Atlantic Monthly* article summarized some of the favored methods. One old timer, swearing by family tradition, recommended washing with "a cup of vinegar with a penny in it," or with vinegar and salt. The household cleaning cupboard was a favorite source of other palliatives such as ammonia, bleach, and potash, which were rubbed into the wounds. One housemaid preferred her newly made soap: "It's got plenty of lye in it . . . I use it on the kitchen sink. . . ."

Gentler remedies came from the pantry and are recorded in magazine articles dating from the early 1900s into the middle of the century. Cool compresses and baths were spiked with cornstarch, baking soda, and oatmeal. Marshmallows, mashed nightshade berries with cream, meat tenderizer, and molasses mixed with sulphur were applied directly to the skin.

The most hopeless cases were treated from the drugstore of the barn. Gasoline, kerosene, and turpentine were rubbed into the afflicted spots. Niter, otherwise known as gunpowder, was rubbed directly onto the skin or mixed with liquids for a healing drink: "It works inside or out." Washes were prepared from 100 percent horse urine.

As scientific research into poison ivy and oak progressed, more sophisticated and sometimes dangerous treatments were developed. Now recognized as a poison itself, sugar of lead (a crystalline form) was a popular pharmaceutical remedy recommended in the 1898 U.S. Department of Agriculture *Farmers' Bulletin no. 86, Thirty Poisonous Plants of the United States.* A 1908 edition included a recipe: "Take alcohol (fifty or seventy-five percent grade) and add as much powdered sugar of lead as can be easily dissolved. This will make a milky fluid which should be rubbed well into the affected skin. Repeat several times in the course of a few days."

The corner druggist was called on to provide ingredients for the sugar of lead recipe and other concoctions for treating "ivy poisoning." McNair's "iron treatment" called for "no more skill than stirring sugar into a cup of coffee." The instructions for preparing a treatment using potassium permanganate in a 5 percent solution with water were equally simple but required a secondary prescription. The treatment left a brown stain on the skin, which was removed with a 1 percent solution of oxalic acid.

All of these remedies probably did the same thing as some of today's topical medicines: They caused the skin to contract, reducing inflammation and thereby relieving the itch. They also provided diversion and a sense of hope that something could be done. Current drugstore medicines bring more predictable relief, and systemic corticosteroids used for severe cases can actually interrupt the allergic process. But now as then a common poison

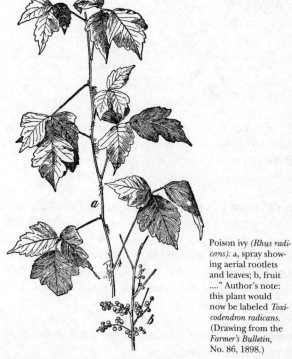

Poison ivy *(Rhus radicans):* a, spray showing aerial rootlets and leaves; b, fruit ...." Author's note: this plant would now be labeled *Toxicodendron radicans.* (Drawing from the *Farmer's Bulletin,* No. 86, 1898.)

Poison oak *(Rhus diversiloba)*, showing leaves, flowers, and fruit...." Author's note: This plant would now be labeled *Toxicodendron pubescens.* (Drawing from the *Farmer's Bulletin,* No. 86, 1898.)

ivy, oak, or sumac allergic reaction will, like the common cold, last about two weeks if you treat it and fourteen days if you do not.

Myths about Poison Ivy, Poison Oak, and Poison Sumac

Myth: I touch it all the time and don't react, so I must be immune.

According to clinical studies only 15 percent of the population is truly immune. Exposed enough times, close enough together, and to enough urushiol, the other 85 percent will react.

Myth: I never touched a plant, but I got a reaction. It must travel through air.

Fact: The oil urushiol is not airborne except in smoke and soot. Some common means of invisible exposure include petting cats and dogs that have roamed through the plants, picking up wood that vines once grew on, and using contaminated tools.

Myth: I get poison ivy whenever it rains.
Fact: The oil urushiol does not travel through rain. It can be present, however, in river or lake water where poison ivy or poison oak leaves and roots trail into the water or in rain gear previously exposed to the plants.

Myth: Drinking the milk of goats that eat poison ivy or oak can make you immune.
Fact: The milk of goats that eat poison ivy or oak has been tested. It does not contain urushiol, therefore it cannot desensitize the body to the oil's presence.

Myth: Eating honey from bees that consume poison ivy, oak, or sumac pollen can make you immune.
Fact: Honey made from such pollen does not contain urushiol and therefore cannot desensitize the body to the oil's presence. (Pollen, flowers, and the pulp of berries do not contain urushiol. All other parts of the plants do, including the skin of the berries.)

Myth: If you've been exposed to poison ivy, oak, or sumac, you can prevent a reaction by washing in very hot or very cold water.
Fact: Washing in a lot of water can dilute urushiol, making it harmless. The temperature of the water does not affect urushiol, but hot water opens the pores, allowing urushiol to penetrate more easily. Tepid water is best because it is kindest to skin. After a reaction has occurred, very hot water can release histamines from the skin and thereby reduce itching. Care must be taken to not burn the skin.

Myth: Eating the leaves can make you immune.
Fact: This dangerous practice can lead to reactions in the mouth, throat, and anus. While theoretically you could become desensitized to urushiol in this way, even the measured doses in allergy shots (not currently available) do not provide predictable relief (see chapter 3).

Myth: If you've been exposed to poison ivy, oak, or sumac, you can prevent a reaction by washing with yellow or brown laundry bar soap.
Fact: Soap, no matter what kind, has no effect on urushiol. Urushiol must either be neutralized by a solvent, such as rubbing alcohol, or diluted with lots of water. Soap will not cause harm as long as it is used with enough water. Used with a small amount of water, soap can spread urushiol.

Myth: Following exposure, washing with the juice of the stem of the wildflower jewelweed (Impatience capensis, Impatience biflora) *can prevent or cure reactions.*
Fact: While jewelweed has a reputation for preventing and curing reactions, scientists have not been able to replicate that success in experimental settings.

Myth: Home remedies are useless.
Fact: Although they have not been proven effective by scientific method, home remedies such as herbal compresses and jewelweed washes bring dramatic relief to some individuals. The mechanism for this is not understood, but as long as the remedy works and causes no harm, it can be used.

Myth: You can spread the rash by scratching it or the blisters.
Fact: No, you cannot. By the time the reaction shows up, urushiol, which causes the rash, is long gone. It bonded with the skin within a few minutes to a few hours of exposure.

*Many years ago I lived as a child in northern Minnesota.
. . . My father pointed out to me the ubiquitous poison ivy,
admonishing me never to touch it. It was quite pretty, actually, beautiful shiny leaves growing together profusely in a
path, like a small religious cult bonded together for company.*

*One afternoon, when I was seven, having nothing better
to do, I rolled in it like a small kitten on a warm, sunny day
cavorting in the grass. About a day or so later, I woke up and
my body was on fire. I had been struck by a biblical plague, I was
certain of it. Blisters appeared all over my body, and the more I
scratched the more blisters there were. Each blister contained a
pale yellow liquid, and when the skin was broken by scratching,
the liquid trickled over my skin causing more blisters.*

*My mother said . . . "It looks as if she has rolled in it!"
"No," said my father. "Poison ivy is very potent, and sometimes
if you stand away from it but in the wind your entire body can
become infected. I do believe that is the case with our Mary Jane."*

*He carefully mixed drops of carbolic acid in a jar of pure
water. "That is poison!" said my mother. "Poison it is but put to
good use!" said my father. "We cannot let the poor child suffer."*

*He dipped cotton into the carbolic acid solution (which, to
me as a child, had a very important odor) and every half hour
or so would gently and carefully daub it over my blisters. A day
or two later, the secretions had dried up, the itching had stopped,
and my epidermis had sloughed off as fine and dry as powder
leaving not a mark or a blemish. My travail had ended.*

*Needless to say I have always had a healthy respect for
poison ivy, and although from that day to this I have not rolled
in it again, I try never to stand downwind of it either. . . .*

–M. S.

*Author's note: There is no urushiol in the rash or blisters,
therefore scratching cannot spread the reaction. And while
urushiol can be carried in smoke, it cannot otherwise travel
through air. Pollen, which can be airborne, does not contain
urushiol.*

The fluid in blisters is made by the body and does not contain urushiol. New rashes are either from the original exposure (some sites take longer to develop) or from new contact with urushiol, perhaps on objects or clothing.

Myth: Scrubbing the skin with ammonia, kerosene, gasoline, or other chemicals will cure a rash.
Fact: Harsh chemicals have no effect on a rash once it is in progress—and they can distress and damage the skin. Washing with a solvent such as rubbing alcohol within a few hours of exposure can prevent a reaction (it neutralizes urushiol and can even leach it out of the skin), but washing with it later than that will have no positive effect.

Myth: It's okay to scratch.
Fact: Scratching a rash or blisters further aggravates the skin and can cause neural (nerve) dermatitis, itching that remains after the reaction is gone. If you cannot resist scratching, see a doctor. Prescription medications can stop the itch.

Myth: Prescription medicines only treat symptoms, not the cause.
Fact: Corticosteroid tablets and injections actually stop the allergic reaction caused by urushiol. Blisters already developed will stop itching, and new ones will not form. The sooner treatment is begun, the faster and more dramatic the relief.

Chapter 3

Chicken Little and the FDA

Poison ivy, oak, and sumac are not to blame for the misery they bring to human beings. The plants themselves are not truly poisonous to us, not in the way of arsenic or certain mushrooms, which are poisons in a classic sense, aggressively attacking every person they encounter, causing injury and even death.

The damage from urushiol comes not from the nature of the oil itself but from the body's allergic reaction to the oil. Like Chicken Little, our immune systems occasionally run amok and declare the sky is falling. A perfectly innocent substance, such as urushiol, is deemed to be a threat to life, and the body sets out to contain and then destroy the villain as though it were a bacterium or a virus. Contact with urushiol can cause one form of allergic reaction called contact dermatitis: a skin rash caused when a substance that can have a toxic effect comes in contact with the skin.

The allergic response to urushiol begins almost immediately upon contact. Within five to ten minutes, the poison oil mixes with lipids, or oils, on the surface of the skin. During that time it is possible to prevent a reaction by washing the skin in copious amounts of water. Small amounts of water—or of anything else, such as disposable hand wipes or the mythologized brown or yellow laundry bar soap—are more likely to spread the urushiol than to remove it.

This fact hardly matters, though. When working or playing outdoors, it is impractical to stop every ten minutes to drown out the invisible urushiol. Besides, every time the skin is washed, the protective oil that floats on it is removed. This oil mixes with urushiol, keeping it away from the skin. When the oil is not present, the urushiol makes direct contact with the skin.

It was formerly thought that once urushiol penetrated into the skin itself, it was impossible to remove it and thereby prevent a reaction. But William L. Epstein, M.D., Dermatology Research at the University of San Francisco in California, reported in *Dermatologic Clinics*, July 1994, that "a window of time (probably 4 to 6 hours) exists when the oil can be leached back out of the skin. . . ." Plain water will not do the trick, even in large quantities, but water mixed with an organic solvent such as acetone or alcohol will. Epstein warned that this wash should not be undertaken until the person has gone indoors for the day. Even more than water alone, the solvents will remove protective oil from the skin, making it more vulnerable to subsequent exposures.

Most of the time people who are allergic to poison ivy, oak, and sumac either do not get to an alcohol wash in time to prevent a reaction or do not even realize they have encountered the dreaded oil. They pack up their contaminated picnic baskets or spin the urushiol-laden tires as they hoist their bikes onto the car rack. And for a day or two, they sleep and work and play unaware that within their bodies a drama intended to preserve life is unfolding into a *film noir*. The urushiol that entered the skin has been spotted by white blood cells, and a three-stage mop-up is under way that will soon be visible as the three stages of a poison ivy, oak, or sumac reaction.

A 1981 U.S. Forest Service pamphlet, prepared by Epstein and V. S. Byers, Ph.D., explains the process. In stage one the skin becomes red and swollen, due to the work of T-lymphocytes, lymphokines, and macrophages. In stage two, about forty-eight hours into the process,

It would never have occurred to me that my experiences with poison ivy as a child would be of any interest to anyone except perhaps my therapist. I was about 9 or 10 years old, living in Kentucky. (After playing in weeds behind our house) I had enormous pus-filled blisters on my forearms from my wrists to my elbows. It was so bad that my mother wrapped my arms with gauze. The blisters would break and the pus would dry on the gauze and then we would have to peel the gauze off and rewrap. I don't recall exactly how long it lasted. It seemed like forever. I think it was about two weeks. This is one of the most vivid memories of my childhood. We treated it with calamine lotion.

The next time I remember having it was on my face. I was at church camp and the camp nurse said she thought it was probably a result of campfire smoke. My face swelled up and my eyes were nearly swelled closed . . . and a fine rash around my lips, eyes, and nostrils. . . .

—B. T.

microblisters begin to form and connect to each other. This is the continuing work of stage-one white cells, plus the addition of mast cells, which release histamines.

About seventy-two hours after the first red dots appear on the skin, stage three is underway. The blisters become large and weepy and, due in part to the swelling and in part to damage to nerves in the area, the real itching begins. In about four days the blisters begin their slow withdrawal, usually lingering for a week or two and sometimes three or more. If urushiol were a germ, it would by this time have been killed by the emergency immune response.

But the human body is not content with one-time crisis control. It has a backup plan. One of the white-cell family members is the T-memory lymphocyte. This clever entity keeps records that any bureaucrat would be proud of. If we get the mumps, it makes a mumps file. The next time a mumps germ appears, the T-memory lymphocyte sounds the alarm, and its other white cell buddies gather round and detain and wipe out the intruder. That is why we get mumps only once in a lifetime. And that is why vaccinations work: Small amounts of known germs are introduced into the body so that T-memory lymphocytes will create recognition codes. If the real germs come along, the body is ready for them. Acting in an orderly and neat fashion, the white cells go after the microscopic bugs as they appear, and we never know that the cleaning crew is at work.

T-memory cells also recall the presence of urushiol and other allergens (things we are allergic to—also called antigens). With allergies, however, an all-out cleanup is usually not initiated until after the body has been sensitized by at least one appearance of the innocent allergen, during which T-memory is accomplished. For reasons unknown, during a later revisit T-memory decides that the harmless allergen should be eliminated. Other white cells are alerted, but they do not proceed in a quiet manner as they do when tracking down germs. Instead they take up the Chicken Little cry and launch an all-out spring cleaning campaign. The more often we are exposed to urushiol, the more anxious T-memory becomes. And with each exposure the scrubbing and routing out by the white cells render the skin more abused.

The whole story, of course, is not that simple. According to Epstein and Byers, urushiol T-memory cells are mortal. If the immune system is not resensitized by frequent exposure, the body can forget that it was ever aware of the oil and may not react again until it is reexposed a number of times. And it appears that as we get older, the Chicken Little side of our immune systems matures and is less likely to react at all to urushiol.

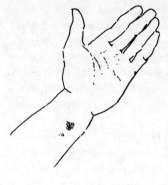

1. In stage one the skin becomes red and swollen due to the work of T-lymphocytes, lymphokines, and macrophages.

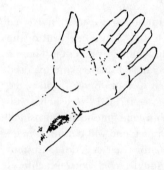

2. In stage two, about forty-eight hours into the process, microblisters begin to form and connect to each other.

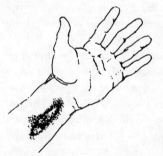

3. In stage three, about seventy-two hours after the first red dots appear, blisters become large and weepy. The real itching begins.
(Illustrations by Misha Beletsky.)

Immunity—or its flip side, sensitivity—to urushiol is therefore difficult to predict. A person may pass freely among the *Toxicodendron* for years without harm and then, for no apparent reason, begin to have reactions. Because of this it is wise not to assume oneself to be permanently immune. Clinical studies conducted by Epstein indicate that only 10 percent of the total U.S. population cannot become sensitized.

The studies, reported in Epstein's *Dermatologic Clinics* article, also indicate that children under the age of five are difficult to sensitize, but that between the ages of six and eight, 85 percent can be experimentally sensitized (they will react to future patch testing).

Among adults the studies show that individual sensitivity varies greatly. Of the 85 to 90 percent of the population vulnerable to urushiol, 50 percent will have a reaction if they brush up against a single plant; exposed to larger amounts, another 30 to 40 percent will react. The final 10 to 15 percent are termed exquisitely sensitive. They will react to minuscule amounts of urushiol, perhaps even on initial contact, and will definitely need to seek medical treatment for their reactions. Epstein also reports that "interestingly, if a person achieves adulthood without succumbing to the allergen, the risk of sensitization falls to approximately 50 percent" (from 85 percent).

With a U.S. population of about 250 million, that means that 125 to 212.5 million souls in the United States are vulnerable to urushiol. Depending on a person's sensitivity and general health of the moment and the amount of oil he or she is exposed to, an individual may have a reaction ranging from a faint rash to extreme swelling and blistering.

Since the urushiol is long gone by the time the first red dots appear, the only thing the victim can do is either

. . . Knowing full well a case of poison oak would delay our return to the hallowed halls (of school), my cousin and I went directly to a patch of poison oak, wiped our arms and legs with the multihued leaves, and picked a bouquet for my mother—naively pretending we did not recognize the evil weed. (My mother must have thought we had adolescent senility.) After a scolding we were told to go wash our hands.

The next day, as expected, I had a mild rash—bumps and lumps soon to be covered with Caladryl. However, my poor cousin Sharon had her eyes swollen shut and resembled a pink puffy blimp. I missed one day of school, and Sharon missed the first week. Of all the poison oak stories in the family, that is the story we cringe to remember and retell.

—K. D.

reduce the symptoms through home and over-the-counter (OTC) treatment (discussed in chapter 4), or interrupt the allergic immune process through the use of prescription medicines such as steroid tablets or injections.

Most dermatologists recommend home and OTC remedies for only the mildest cases. Blisters that cause intense itching warrant a visit to the doctor's office. Blistering that involves the face, the genitals, or large areas of any part of the body should definitely be treated medically to prevent scarring and hasten recovery.

Corticosteroids are the treatment of choice for a reaction to urushiol. A prescription strength gel may be offered to help dry up less-weepy blisters (which do not contain urushiol and do not spread the rash), but the real remedy comes in the form of corticosteroid pills or injections. Rather than treating only the symptoms, these systemic corticosteroids (which treat the whole body system) actually interrupt the allergic process. Epstein and Byers, in the U.S. Forest Service pamphlet, explain that if the

. . . Over time I discovered that the very best palliative, bar none, is to take the hottest, high-force shower I can tolerate several times a day, aiming the nozzle directly at my rash sites. The relief of burning water on the unbearable itching is ecstasy and seems to numb the itching for an hour or so. . . .

. . . In 1971, when I was nineteen and working as a forest firefighter . . . we were assigned to a big one . . . in the Los Padres National Forest (California). The steep hillsides there are lousy with poison oak, and we had to cut fire breaks through it day and night; there was no way to avoid it the way you can when on a genteel day hike. After nearly a week "on the line" I looked like the elephant man. . . . My wrists were so swollen they filled the fully open, expandable sleeves of my Nomex fire shirt. One eye was sealed shut and the other barely open. Plains and ridges of blisters covered my midsection from crotch to nipples, extending over my shoulders and wrapping my flanks under my arms to my back—an epidermal continent of misery. My waist was raw from rubbing against my clothing. My thighs and calves, constantly rubbing and abrading each other, were girdled with a blistering, leaky rash. As soon as we got to base camp, I was put in an official station wagon and hauled off to a hospital for a steroid shot . . . and a useless bottle of calamine lotion. . . .

—B. O.

Author's note: After a rash has erupted, very hot water can release histamines from the skin and thereby relieve itching, sometimes for many hours. Care must be taken to not burn the skin.

corticosteroids are given before the rash turns to blisters, blisters will not form. If they are given after blisters form, no new ones will develop, but the old ones will take the usual time to resolve.

For about 75 percent of cases, says Epstein, corticosteroid tablets given in decreasing doses over a week or two may be enough to preempt the reaction. For others, especially those with severe reactions, he recommends aggressive treatment with an initial corticosteroid injection followed by two days of dosing with pills. If the reaction starts to erupt again after the pills are discontinued, they can be taken again for one day, and again for one day several times more, if necessary, until the eruptions cease.

Even with the availability and effectiveness of corticosteroids, however, prevention is still the best medicine. After my first bout with the rash, I vowed to never again be exposed to the demon leaf. "Fat chance," my friends told me. And they were right. Even if I didn't go outdoors, I could still get a rash from petting the dog—and I did.

Despair brought on by similar experiences is possibly behind the rather extreme measure reported in the lore of aboriginal Americans of the United States and Mexico: the eating of poison ivy and oak leaves to obtain immunity. While there appears to be no documentation that this was ever common practice, it is theoretically possible for it to work, in the same way that allergy shots do. Naturalist Ewell Gibbons, in his 1962 book, *Stalking the Wild Asparagus*, said that he heard about lumberjacks in the Pacific Northwest who had adopted the practice. He tried it himself, since his forest peregrinations sometimes led to mild rashes. Beginning in early spring, he ate three leaflets a day for three weeks, then stopped. The growing size of the leaflets provided him with a gradually increasing dose, as is common with allergy shots. For the two springs that Gibbons tried this, he had no poison ivy reactions.

American Indians today, when questioned by Epstein, eschewed the idea of eating poison ivy or oak leaves. The practice was not part of their contemporary culture.

*In my childhood I was susceptible to poison ivy in the extreme.
. . . On my sixteenth birthday I was bedfast with a leg swollen
to twice its size with the allergic reaction.*

*I was visiting grandparents south of Indianapolis in a
preteen summer, when I got into poison ivy and someone suggested I get some "blacksmith water," a term I understood well.
This was about 1940. There were two blacksmiths in town.
. . . Every operation of theirs fascinated me, including seeing
and hearing red hot metal being dipped into a vat of water.
Using that water on the blisters seemed to dry them up faster
than usual, certainly faster than toughing it out.*

*In later years another outbreak got me to the doctor, who
prescribed "10 percent tincture of iron in glycerine," a link to
the blacksmith I could not miss. . . .*

—D. P.

Other home-style attempts to produce immunity
include eating honey made by bees that consume poison ivy or oak pollen and drinking milk from goats that
eat the leaves. However, the pollen of the toxic trio does
not contain urushiol; it therefore cannot carry it into the
honey and therefore cannot induce immunity. Similarly,
the urushiol consumed by goats does not test as present
in their milk.

For nearly a century, medical science has tried to
improve on these urushiol munchables as a way to avoid
poison ivy or oak dermatitis. In 1919, a Philadelphia physician named Schamberg concocted the first poison ivy
allergy extract. He tested it in both oral and injectable
forms. E. Sue Watson, Ph.D., in a 1986 article in *Clinics
in Dermatology*, described the long and torturous process
from that first approach until around 1983. The first anecdotal reports around 1919 claimed a 95 percent success

rate, but between then and 1942, scientific review offered contradictory information. In 1926 the Council on Pharmacy and Chemistry, Watson reported, "admitted *Rhus* (*Toxicodendron*) preparations into *New and Nonofficial Remedies*," but rescinded its sanction around 1942 "due to lack of proof of efficacy and reports of severe adverse reactions and sometimes exacerbation of active cases. . . ."

In 1944, with the war still on, I was sent to complete my high schooling at a private military academy in the Shenandoah Valley of Virginia. We ROTC "cadets" had very serious weekend "Field Training" on land the school owned near Waynesbro, Virginia. It was fall, and the apple orchards in which we played at war were covered with all sorts of reddish leaves. We did not realize until two days later that over two hundred of us teenage boys had been lying and crawling about over dense poison ivy and poison sumac all afternoon.

That night a group of senior cadets about to be transferred over to the regular U.S. Army decided to sow some last wild oats and somehow managed to get a local prostitute into the school. . . . Word spread that this situation was . . . open to all. . . . There was no real count as to how many boys had contact with her. The numbers grew with each retelling.

Two days later absolute panic struck the Cadet Corps as rashes and blisters were appearing on the private parts of any cadet who had urinated while lying down in these poisonous orchards. . . . It was universally assumed that all these boys had contracted some kind of dire venereal disorder.

. . . There was talk of suicide, of running away to the Navy, etc., until the school nurse, a salty old gal, laughingly identified the rashes for what they were. This is the only anecdote I have ever encountered about poison ivy in which those who contracted it . . . (found) the diagnosis a great joy and relief.

—*J. G.*

The council, however, had no power to enforce its opinion, and beginning in 1928 separate poison ivy and poison oak allergy extracts were licensed by the Federal Drug Administration (FDA). In 1976 combined poison ivy and oak extracts were licensed. Injectables were generally administered once annually, late in the winter. Capsules were usually taken several times a day in increasing doses, usually for several months beginning at the time of expected exposure.

Both processes produced immunity in some people, but both also continued to produce side effects, including *pruritus ani*—intense anal itching, caused by the extract being excreted in feces. The shots also sometimes resulted in scarring at the injection site. While the capsules were generally believed to be more effective with fewer side effects, the demanding regimen made them less useful.

Over the decades scientists continued their efforts to make poison ivy and oak allergy shots more effective and friendly. In 1984 *Time* magazine reported the imminent release of a refined vaccine that would not produce *pruritus ani*. The promise, however, never came to pass. A 1992 report in the *New York Times* that a new vaccine was about to be tested also proved to be premature.

This troubled history of our determined effort to slay the urushiol dragon is reflected in current reviews and actions by the FDA. In 1983, at the direction of Congress, the FDA began a review of all biologic products—those made from natural substances as opposed to those made from chemicals. Among the products on the review list were the poison ivy/oak oral and injectable allergenic extracts that had been licensed in one form or another since the 1920s.

In 1985 the review report classified the extract for shots in Category 3B: Insufficient data and unfavorable ratio of benefit to risk. Unless the companies producing

Back in 1926 I was afflicted with poison ivy while visiting my uncle's farm in New Jersey. I still remember the mortification I experienced when my mother and aunt decided to apply compresses to my face that were soaked in my uncle's urine. It was my understanding only male urine was suitable because women menstruated.

—M. L.

the extract provided new data to prove the product "safe, effective, and consistent," licensure to produce it would be revoked. The oral drug was eventually classified in Category 1: Safe and effective. But it did not meet consistency standards in lot release. This meant that if the companies wanted to continue manufacturing the drug, they would have to provide data showing that each lot produced was similar to every other lot according to certain guidelines.

By August 1993, manufacturers of the extracts had not provided new data and were prohibited from releasing any more of the products into the market. A recall was not issued; extracts still in pharmacies or doctors' offices could be used. Around that time the American Public Health Association sued in an effort to force compliance with the 1985 report, and on December 16, 1994, licenses for the injections were revoked, and permission to distribute the oral extracts was withdrawn. Until those rulings are reversed, or new data is presented, neither the oral capsules nor the allergy immunizations will be available.

This does not mean that the FDA disapproves of the extracts in general. It does mean that no manufacturer is, at the moment, willing to do the testing and control necessary to maintain licensure. Urushiol is not deadly, and deaths related to it are usually attributed to other complications of illnesses or treatments, not to an

Sensitivity/Immunity to Urushiol, the Allergenic Oil in Poison Ivy, Poison Oak, and Poison Sumac

Data derived from clinical (experimental) studies*.

Status	Possible Explanations	Potential for Change
Never react.	• Are under the age of six. • Have not been sensitized (exposed to urushiol). • Achieved adulthood without reaction (risk falls from 85% to 50%). • Are among the 10 to 15% of the population who appear to be truly immune.	Unless truly immune, can still react if adequately sensitized and exposed.
Didn't react formerly, but do now.	• Are among the 85% of the population vulnerable to urushiol. • Not previously exposed often enough to maintain sensitization (it can wear off). • Not previously exposed to a large enough quantity to trigger reaction (varies with individuals).	Can become less sensitive if exposure is lessened or absent long enough.
Usually react. Reactions vary from mild to severe.	• Are among the 30 to 40% who are mildly sensitive (react to more than 2 micrograms, the approximate amount in one crushed leaf). • Degree of any given reaction depends on amount of urushiol and individual sensitivity.	Can become less sensitive if exposure is lessened or absent long enough.

Always react. Reactions often severe.	• Are among the 50% of the population that is very sensitive (reacts to about 2 micrograms, the approximate amount in one crushed leaf). • Degree of any given reaction depends on amount of urushiol and individual sensitivity.	Can become less sensitive if exposure is lessened or absent long enough.
Always react. Reactions always severe and usually require medical attention.	• Are among the 15% of the population who are exquisitely sensitive (react to as little as 1 microgram).	Can become less sensitive if exposure is decreased, but will regain extreme sensitivity if frequent exposure resumes.
Used to react, but now don't.	• Are among the 85% of the population vulnerable to urushiol. • Previously exposed to large enough quantity of urushiol to sensitize and trigger a reaction (varies with individuals), but now contact is reduced or absent.	Can be resensitized if exposed often enough.

*Based on studies by William L. Epstein, M.D., professor of dermatology, Dermatology Research, University of California, San Francisco

When I was a child in the early 1920s, when my brother and I got poison ivy from playing in the woods in the northwest part of the Bronx (New York City) where we grew up, the remedy was first to scrub the affected area with brown laundry soap and then smear on glycerin and then shake on powdered sulphur. This was covered with gauze wrappings. It was messy and smelly and only somewhat effective.

—B. H.

urushiol reaction itself. But clearly the need for safe and effective means of immunizing against urushiol reactions still exists. In addition to causing individual suffering and incapacity, urushiol reactions are the most common cause of dermatitis-related workers' compensation claims.

Other poison ivy and poison oak products also warrant production. Epstein, during research conducted for the U.S. Forest Service, designed a patch testing kit that grades individual sensitivity to urushiol. This would make it easy to identify individuals who are exquisitely sensitive and therefore should not engage in frontline forest fire work, as well as those who are mildly sensitive and should use protective clothing and other measures. The test would work equally well for other outdoor workers, such as utility line persons, park employees, and loggers, and for outdoor researchers and recreationists. The kit could also be used to detect changes in an individual's sensitivity.

Here is a home remedy I've heard of that cures poison ivy: The person who is afflicted is to be rubbed down on the infected areas with his or her own urine. Pretty disgusting procedure, however I've heard it works like a charm. . . .

—B. T.

Poison ivy *(Toxicodendron radicans)* vine growing next to Virginia Creeper vine (five leaflets, next to yellow flower).   PHOTO BY DR. THOMAS HEMMERLY

Rydberg's poison ivy *(Toxicodendron rydbergii).*   PHOTO BY DR. THOMAS HEMMERLY

Poison ivy *(Toxicodendron radicans)*,
climbing form in autumn color.
PHOTO BY DR. THOMAS HEMMERLY

Western poison oak *(Toxicodendron diversi-lobum)*, climbing form. Note that leaflets
are unlobed variation of usual lobed shape.
PHOTO BY DR. DAVID KEIL.

Western poison oak *(Toxicodendron diversilobum)*, shrub form.
PHOTO BY MR. PAUL KULD

Western poison oak *(Toxicodendron diversilobum),* climbing form.   PHOTO BY DR. DAVID KEIL

Eastern poison oak *(Toxicodendron pubescens).*   PHOTO FROM MISSOURI BOTANICAL GARDEN
ARCHIVES, EDGAR DENISON COLLECTION.

Poison sumac *(Toxicodendron vernix)* leaves.   PHOTO BY DR. THOMAS HEMMERLY.

Flowers of poison oak *(Toxicodendron diversilobum)*.   PHOTO BY DR. DAVID KEIL.

Berries of Rydberg's poison ivy *(Toxicodendron rydbergii)*. Berries of poison ivies and oaks are nearly identical.
PHOTO BY DR. MARSHALL SUNDBERG.

. . . I found the following therapy to work the best for me. I would get into the shower and train the hot water directly on the involved spot. This would cause a tremendous release from the itch fibers (it would practically cause me to go weak at the knees). I would then turn the water hotter, causing another release. I would continue to turn up the water temperature until no further release would occur, following which I would experience relief for up to eight hours. . . . As a practicing emergency physician, I am somewhat reluctant to prescribe this anecdotal therapy, particularly since there is the danger of burning oneself if care is not taken. The result has been dramatic for me the few times I have had occasion to use it.

—*R. C.*

Author's note: Very hot water can release histamines from the skin and thereby relieve itching, sometimes for many hours. Care must be taken to not burn the skin.

Chapter 4

The Demon Itch

In the United States poison ivy is more than a plant. It is a popular culture icon. The 1959 song "Poison Ivy," warbled by the Coasters, warned that sufferers would need to stock up on Calamine lotion. The tune made it to number seven on the pop charts.

Itch is the common denominator in poison ivy as metaphor, parable, or threat. The reason for any itching sensation, says the *American Medical Association Encyclopedia of Medicine*, "is not fully understood." We do know, however, that it comes along with the swelling and inflammation that accompany skin rashes, including that of poison ivy and oak. While it may seem that the urushiol itch is more intense and perverse than other allergic skin reactions, William L. Epstein, M.D., professor of dermatology, Dermatology Research, University of California, San Francisco, says that any allergic contact dermatitis can present an itch just as distressing, including reactions to nickel—the second most common skin allergen after urushiol.

Except in extreme cases that involve swelling of the face or other sensitive areas, without the itch no one would care much about poison ivy or oak rashes. The impetus for treatment comes from the desire to rend one's flesh from one's body. We all know we shouldn't do that. Scratching does bring momentary relief, but also further ravages the already damaged skin.

Short of being hog-tied, however, we are likely to yield to our baser impulses unless the itch itself can be stopped or at least lessened. Like our forebears who turned to gunpowder and sugar of lead, we will rub almost anything on our hide in our quest for peace. Most conversations about poison ivy or oak will produce a list of foolproof home remedies. The more extreme measures range from coating the blisters with nail polish or deodorant to removing the infected skin layer by scrubbing with brushes and alcohol.

Most home remedies are more sane and include cooling compresses, hot showers, and herbal poultices. A favorite topical treatment is the application of the juice of *Impatience biflora*, jewelweed. This common swamp and ditchside plant was used medicinally by American Indians and is still pronounced a sure cure by many urushiol victims. The intrepid naturalist Ewell Gibbons kept mash of jewelweed ice cubes in his freezer for winter and early spring urushiol emergencies.

The reputation for the success of this natural, no-side-effects, cost-free remedy has for generations outlasted medical skepticism about the chemical effect of the plant on poison ivy or oak rashes. An article in the *Journal of Wilderness Medicine* in 1991 reported that, in an experimental setting, the use of *Impatience biflora* as a preventive or treatment for urushiol dermatitis did not duplicate the success related in personal anecdotes. Yet the actual effect of it and other home remedies on some individuals cannot be denied: Claims of relief and cures are not uncommon.

The explanation for this discrepancy between experiments and experience invokes a phenomenon called the placebo effect: Through an unknown process the body appears to accept the suggestion that it will get well—and does. Testing of prescription drugs prior to licensure by the FDA includes placebo testing, and for most drugs, 15 to 30 percent of participants obtain relief from placebos that is similar to or the same as relief gained from the real drug.

What does this mean? My first reaction is a mixture of embarrassment and denial. I don't like being fooled, even by myself. But the authors of *The Healing Brain* consider the placebo effect to be a tool of the mind used to promote health: "The (placebo) process works . . . because the human body is its own best apothecary and because the most successful prescriptions are those that are filled by the body itself."

Mind over body is not a new idea. Hypnosis, perhaps the ultimate power of suggestion, has been successfully used in place of anesthesia in dentistry and other medical settings. Meditation can help lower blood pressure, and spontaneous remission of such diverse ailments from cancer to warts is sometimes attributed to a change in attitude or emotion.

Perhaps when human beings are given the promise of hope and comfort, the immune system is freed up to do its work. Perhaps there is some not yet understood chemical process triggered by a sense of well-being. Epstein speculates that the placebo effect allows or causes the secretion of some beneficial substance, and he encourages poison ivy and oak patients to use home remedies that work for them.

Another explanation might apply to some cases of poison ivy or oak home cures. The urushiol reaction is

The 1985 movie Poison Ivy *stars Michael J. Fox and Nancy McKeon in a summer camp frolic, and poison ivy plays itself. In the 1992 movie of the same title, however, a poisonous Ivy is played by Drew Barrymore. In eighty-nine minutes the human version of the noxious weed ruins both a summer and a family.*

self-limiting: It has a natural course and eventually re-solves itself whether or not anything is done to treat it. Sometimes credit is given to a home cure that should go to what Brian Livermore, M.D., Ph.D., of the Northern Medical Clinic in Bemidji, Minnesota, calls "tincture of time."

Misunderstandings about cures for urushiol reactions are outnumbered only by misunderstandings about the rash itself, how it spreads on the body, and how to treat it at home. From an 1898 *Farmers' Bulletin* to a 1991 book on weeds to Internet chatter, the information is often contradictory (wash in hot water, wash in cold water) and misleading (scratching the blisters will spread the rash), or downright inadvisable (scrub the skin vigorously). Wo-ven in among the errors are accurate and helpful bits of information.

It has taken decades of study and experience to sort out the mix. A 1923 article in *Outing* magazine declared that "the wind carries the spores of the poison, and some people become poisoned when standing several yards away from the plant itself." Wrong. There is no urushiol in the spores (pollen) of the plant, although urushiol from burning plants can be carried in smoke.

Later in the article: "Gasoline is one of the best pre-ventive measures." Right idea, wrong substance. Gasoline is too harsh for the already vulnerable skin. Alcohol is better (rubbing alcohol works) and can achieve the same

Entertainment subcultures, such as the world of rockabilly, recognize the value of a universal image. A 1990 Rolling Stones review describes Poison Ivy Rorschach as the "all burr and bristle" guitarist for the Cramps, a group that started scratching the itch of rockhounds in 1971.

result: If used within about four hours of exposure, it can actually leach the urushiol out of the skin.

And later still: If no other remedies are available "rub the hands with moist earth." Wrong. This would not provide enough material to dilute the oil into impotency and could therefore spread the oil.

What *should* you do? The following considerations are derived from conversations with half a dozen dermatologists, family practice physicians, and researchers and are corroborated by recent articles in scientific journals.

Preventing Contact

The *Outing* article declares, "You can never trust poison ivy. It strikes without rhyme or reason." To anyone who has ever tried to avoid contact, the statement has the ring of truth. But the real truth is that to get poison ivy or oak dermatitis you must come in contact with the oil, either through touching the plant, through contamination by urushiol-laden smoke, or by touching an object or an animal that carries the urushiol.

This can occur by petting the dog or handling a contaminated rake handle. But the possibilities are endless. Wallace Wanek, Ph.D., professor of biology at Bemidji State University in Minnesota, tells of a friend who got the rash from seeds in the crop of a grouse he was cleaning. Another friend contacted it from the innards of a deer.

While complete avoidance of urushiol may not be possible, there are still many ways to minimize contact with it. If you are going into the great outdoors, dress appropriately. (Poison sumac usually confines itself to deep swamps and is not easily encountered.) Wear shoes and socks, not open sandals. Look carefully at plants before touching or wading through them (see chapter 1 for identification tips). If you are going to be digging roots in a poison ivy or oak area, wear gloves.

If you sweat from heat or hard work or both, be especially cautious about wiping sweat from your forehead with your arm. If you've gotten urushiol on your bare arm or shirt sleeve you can transfer it to the sweat on your forehead; it can run down onto your face and even into your eyes. This is a serious problem for forest fire workers. Epstein recommends wearing a sweatband on the forehead to help prevent this kind of exposure.

Sweat can also transport urushiol through clothing—outside to inside through the woven cloth—and deposit the oil on skin. Oil carried in sweat that runs inside of gloves or boots or is caught around a waistband is especially likely to cause a reaction. The confinement promotes bonding with the skin. Wear loose clothing.

Also watch out for water laced with urushiol. Although it is unusual, plants growing on the edge of a river or lake can release enough urushiol into the water to cause a reaction. Epstein tells of a number of people who have had poison oak reactions on their legs and arms after walking in muddy floodwaters. Don't walk, swim, or wash close to the shore where poison ivy or oak grows.

It is especially important that you avoid contact with urushiol-laden smoke. Know what kind of wood you are using on a campfire, and do not burn poison ivy, oak, or sumac in an effort to eradicate it. Even old, dried vines and roots contain urushiol that can be carried in smoke; the smoke can settle anywhere on the body and can be inhaled as well. One forest fire fighter, who suffered exposure to both urushiol-rich sweat and smoke, described himself as an "epidermal continent of misery."

. . . Back in the early 1940s, mother would go to the pharmacy and buy potassium permanganate. For some inexplicable reason she would put this very purple stuff in the palm of her left hand and dab it with cotton over all the itchy spots on my brother and me, leaving a quite permanent purple stain. One year when I was about three years old and my brother nine, he and I managed to have poison ivy literally from head to toe,. We spent a fairly reclusive summer with purple bodies—and my mother with a deep purple stain in the palm of her left hand the size of a silver dollar, attesting to a mother's sacrifice. This cure also kept playmates away, as we were considered too strange. . . . Given some of my mother's home remedies, this one was benign!

—*L. S.*

If you have pets that travel through poison ivy or oak patches, wash them frequently in copious amounts of water. Epstein recommends dunking them in a tub (wear gloves and wash yourself with copious amounts of water afterward).

Ivy Block™ is a barrier cream that came on the market in 1996. It is spread on the skin prior to exposure to urushiol and contains quaternium-18 bentonite, a chemical that bonds with urushiol. This prevents urushiol from bonding with the skin. IvyBlock™ is the only barrier cream with ingredients approved by the FDA for the prevention of urushiol dermatitis. A 1995 study by Marks showed that quarternium-18 bentonite prevented a reaction 68 per cent of the time. When a reaction occurred, it was much less severe. However, a barrier cream does not take the place of caution. Learn the *Toxicodendron* species in your area (see chapter 1).

Damage Control

If you have been outside and have seen a suspicious leaf, assume that urushiol is on you or something you have brought home. Epstein tells of a study where a tracer dye was placed on hand equipment used by forest fire fighters. At the end of a day, the dye revealed that urushiol had spread from the blade of an axe all the way to the tip of the handle.

If you think you have been exposed, you might be able to minimize the damage by washing in copious amounts of water. But—despite the fact that urushiol begins to bond with the skin within five to ten minutes of exposure—do not try to wash it off while you are still in danger of being exposed to it. Washing the skin removes protective oils that help keep urushiol away from your skin.

When you are done for the day, try to decontaminate yourself and your belongings. Wash everything—your clothes, your car tires, your body—in copious amounts of water. While urushiol is an oil and therefore does not dissolve in water, sufficient amounts will dilute it, making it harmless. You can use soap or even gasoline on objects if you also rinse them with plenty of water, however, gasoline should not be used on the skin.

I am a retired Visiting Nurse who worked with the V.N.S.N.Y. in Queens in New York City. On a first visit to a community of rather small one-family houses near LaGuardia Airport where my patient, an elderly widow, lived alone, I approached the house admiring its neatly clipped hedge which surrounded a small front yard. As I reached the gate, thinking how nicely the hedge had been cut, I realized to my horror that the entire hedge was of poison ivy.

—D. S.

To cleanse your poor mortal flesh, start by swabbing it with a cloth drenched in rubbing alcohol. You don't have to rub it in. Just pass the cloth over your skin. Then, right after the alcohol wash, take a long shower, washing with a lot of plain water. Use soap if you want, as long as there is plenty of water. Using laundry bar soap won't provide more relief or protection than any other soap. Do not scrub or otherwise assault your skin. When cleaning up after exposure to urushiol, keep your shower water at a comfortable temperature. Hot water will remove more oil, but is hard on the skin and also opens the skin's pores making them more receptive to urushiol.

Rash Patches and Weepy Blisters

You stuck to the forest path. You took off your clothes and dropped them promptly into the washing machine. You doused yourself with rubbing alcohol. You showered.

The next morning you wake up scratching your arms. Forget about taking another shower. Forget about using more rubbing alcohol. Urushiol has bonded with your skin. You are past the prevention stage. Prepare yourself for a grisly game of poison ivy or poison oak roulette.

First, do not worry about spreading the urushiol by scratching the itch. When it bonded with your skin, it changed chemically; it is no longer urushiol. If new patches appear over the next several days, either they developed from the first exposure, taking longer to do so because there was less oil at that site, or you have made fresh contact with urushiol. The strings of rash seen pulling away from blisters are not the result of your scratching, but rather are the pattern of the original urushiol contamination, often caused by a leaf drawn across the skin.

If you've had serious reactions in the past, or if the rash is clearly developing on your face or genitals or large areas of your body, go to the doctor right away. You will probably be offered prescription corticosteroids, either in pills or by injection. They do have side effects, but for many people those are a lesser evil than the reaction itself. If the drugs make you feel bad, Epstein recommends that you take to your bed and let your body and the drugs do their work.

I want to relate to you my experience with poison ivy sixty years ago.... When I was eighteen years old I developed the worst case of poison ivy the doctor had ever seen. I had this red, angry rash from the tip of my head down to the tips of my toes. The worst part of this ailment is that I had it in my ears, and I developed blisters, and the blisters, besides being itchy, were pulsating....

[At the hospital clinic] the intern diagnosed my rash as "poison ivy" and told me it was the worse case he had ever seen. [He] just gave me a bottle of calamine lotion and told me to apply to affected areas as often as necessary.... Needless to say, the lotion did not expedite the healing process.

The one thing I could say in its favor is that as I applied it, I was able to scratch myself—it was sheer ecstasy—but it was only for a moment, for as soon as I stopped, the throbbing, itching, and burning began once more. I also remember standing by the open window, as I thought a breeze would lessen the torture. At that time I thought how nice it would be if I had the strength to throw myself off (I lived on the fourth floor)....

In three weeks I was recovered, and I have never had a recurrence of "poison ivy." I have had since then a Cesarean for the birth of my two daughters, hysterectomy, several bone fractures—but I always look back to that affliction as the most painful one I ever had.

—L. S.

If the rash is mild or limited (75 percent of cases, says Epstein), you can try to treat it at home. The little red bumps seen on the first day or so indicate that the allergic immune process is underway. Topical OTC creams that contain cortisone might help relieve the itch. If herbal or other home remedies work for you, this is the time to start them. Just remember that your skin is delicate and has a tough and important job—to protect the whole inside of your body. Treat it kindly. No fingernail brushes, dishwasher powder, or other aggressions.

As the reaction progresses, the rash turns to blisters, which then break and weep. The watery fluid is only blood serum. It does not contain urushiol and therefore cannot spread the rash. If new rash spots are appearing now, you may still have some urushiol around your house or on your shoes or other objects, such as your camera. Or, according to some immunologists, the rash may be spreading through your lymph system. This notion has not been confirmed, but it does fit with the experience of some people. Epstein also notes that occasionally any dermatitis episode can trigger neural dermatitis—a reactivation of a rash at an old dermatitis site.

Assuming you are not reinfecting yourself with unbonded urushiol lurking on a shoelace, your home treatment will change a bit with the appearance of the blisters. If they are especially distressing, it is not too late to go to the doctor for help. Corticosteroids even now will interrupt the immune process. A corticosteroid injection will even prevent new blisters from forming, although ones already present will continue their course toward resolution.

If you are sticking with the bathroom medicine cabinet, now is the time to break out the calamine. It will help dry up the weepy sores, making them less itchy. Cool or tepid wet compresses of plain water, Burrow's Solution, or colloidal oatmeal will still help as well. Some aficionados recommend very hot compresses, baths, or showers. Care must be taken to not burn the skin, but treatment of the rash with hot water can bring relief that sometimes lasts for hours. The hot water draws histamines, the cause of some of the itching, to and away from the surface of the skin, but it also taxes the skin's integrity, opening pores and making it generally more vulnerable. As noted earlier, hot water should not be used to cleanse the skin immediately after exposure to urushiol.

If you go the old tried-and-true route of calamine lotion (it is an ingredient of many OTC products), make sure you are using calamine and not caladryl. Caladryl contains the antihistamine Benadryl, which does not significantly increase relief and can sensitize the body to Benadryl, increasing the possibility of future allergic reactions to that very important drug. Antihistamines are rarely prescribed for urushiol reactions, says Epstein, because there is very little histamine release in their course.

If the itching gets to you, and you just have to scratch, it's a good idea to have a doctor treat the itch even if your reaction is not severe. Scratching only brings temporary—though ecstatic—relief and can cause neural (nerve) dermatitis. This after-dermatitis itch can hang on for weeks and even months after the urushiol reaction is healed. It should be diagnosed and treated by a physician.

Emergency Situations

Most urushiol reactions can be borne without medical attention. However, if you know you have been exposed to urushiol-laden smoke, or if you experience skin or lung reactions that could be from such smoke, a call or trip to the local hospital emergency room or urgent care center is warranted. Urushiol is not visible in smoke, nor does it

1. Prevention

What To Do	Why	See Chapter
Learn to identify *Toxicodendrons*.	Prevention is the best medicine.	1
Dress to protect your skin.	Urushiol begins to bond with skin within 5 to 10 minutes.	4
Do not wipe your forehead or face with sleeves, arms, or hands.	Urushiol can be transferred to sweat on your brow and face.	4
Wear a sweatband on your forehead.	Urushiol-laden sweat can drip onto your face and into your eyes.	4
If you relieve yourself in the woods, do not pick a handful of leaves to cleanse yourself.	Yes, the worst can and does happen.	4
Keep pets from wandering in poison ivy or poison oak.	You can get a reaction from urushiol carried on pet fur.	2, 4
Consider using the barrier cream IvyBlock™.	To keep urushiol away from skin.	4
At home and when traveling, keep a piece of cloth in a generous container of rubbing alcohol.	Use it to swab your skin after exposure to urushiol—then wash in copious amounts of water. If you are in the woods, a river or lake will do—but avoid water where poison ivy or oak grows on the bank.	4 and Chart 2 below
If poison ivy or oak is growing on a riverbank or lakeshore, do not swim, walk, or wash in nearby water.	Although it is not common, urushiol can be present in a concentration high enough to cause a reaction.	4
Do not burn any part of poison ivy, oak, or sumac plants, even if they are dead.	Urushiol is carried in smoke and can react in the mouth, lungs, eyes, and ears and on skin.	4

2. Damage Control After Exposure

What To Do	Why	See Chapter
Wait to wash until done with outdoor work or play session.	Washing removes protective skin oils.	4
If it has been less than 4 to 6 hours since exposure, gently swab skin with rubbing alcohol.	Alcohols can leach urushiol out of the skin for up to 4 to 6 hours after exposure.	4
Do not wash with prepackaged alcohol wipes.	They do not contain enough alcohol and may spread urushiol.	4
Wash in copious amounts of water.	Large quantities of water can dilute urushiol on the skin.	4
Do not wash in ordinary amounts of water.	Small amounts of water can spread urushiol on the skin.	4
Wash your entire body and your hair.	Urushiol can wick through wet or sweat-soaked clothing.	4
Use soap if you want to, but only with copious amounts of water.	Soap, including yellow laundry bar soap, can spread urushiol unless used with a lot of water.	2, 4
Use gentle home-cleaning remedies. Do not do mean things to your skin, like washing it with gasoline or scrubbing it vigorously.	Don't abuse your skin. It won't help, and the urushiol will do enough damage on its own.	2, 4
Wash clothes and objects that might carry urushiol with copious amounts of water.	Urushiol can stay active on objects for years.	4

3. If Rash Appears

What To Do	Why	See Chapter
Forget about washing urushiol off your skin—it's long gone.	Urushiol breaks down when it bonds with the skin.	4
Check household, car, and outdoor equipment for objects that might still be contaminated.	One rash is enough—you don't need to reexpose yourself.	2, 4
If you are extremely sensitive, see your doctor immediately.	Immediate treatment can stop the reaction from progressing further.	3
Treat mild itching with cortisone creams and/or wet compresses and/or soothing, gentle home remedies.	These can help reduce itching.	3, 4
Do not reapply alcohol or other astringents.	Your skin has enough trouble already.	3, 4
Try not to scratch; if the itching becomes unbearable, call your doctor.	Scratching can cause "after-dermatitis itch"; prescription medicines can bring relief.	3, 4

4. As the Reaction Progresses

What To Do	Why	See Chapter
When the rash starts to blister, apply lotions that contain calamine.	Calamine dries the blisters, which helps reduce itching.	4
Don't worry about the oozing fluid.	This is from blood serum and does not contain urushiol.	3
If the itching becomes unbearable, see your doctor.	Prescription drugs can interrupt the reaction—and the itching.	4
If gentle home remedies work for you, continue to use them.	They can help relieve the itch.	3, 4
Continue to use wet compresses.	They can help relieve the itch.	4
Do not further abuse your skin by applying abrasive substances.	It won't help.	4

5. Emergency Situations

What To Do	Why	See Chapter
If smoke from burning poison ivy, oak, or sumac is inhaled, seek immediate medical treatment.	Urushiol can react in the trachea and lungs; immediate treatment is highly successful.	3, 4
If reaction involves the face, eyes, genitals, or large areas of the body, seek immediate medical treatment.	Early treatment can stop the reaction, bring relief, and help prevent scarring.	3, 4

have an odor, but a reaction in the trachea or lungs can be serious. The smoke can also land on the skin and even get into the eyes and ears. Immediate treatment with corticosteroids can interrupt the allergic reaction and prevent complications.

Any urushiol reaction that involves the face, genitals, or large areas of the body should be treated medically. Corticosteroids not only bring relief but can prevent scarring.

Homemade Poison Ivy and Oak Prevention Kit

Here is an inexpensive and effective way to prevent a poison ivy or oak reaction. If you are a hiker or camper, keep this kit in your car or with your camping gear.

Fill a pint or quart jar with rubbing alcohol. Cut a washcloth in half and keep one part in the jar. After exposure to poison ivy or poison oak, remove the cloth from the jar and slosh the rubbing alcohol on exposed skin (but not the face), then rinse with a lot of water. No need to scrub—just slosh, Return the cloth to the jar for next time.

For up to several hours after exposure, using rubbing alcohol this way will neutralize the urushiol, thereby preventing a reaction. Water alone can only dilute the oil and must be used within ten to twenty minutes of exposure. Soap, including Fels Naphtha, does not affect urushiol and can, in fact, spread the oil if not used with enough water.

Chapter 5

Foreign Lands and Farmer Birds

Humans have been afflicted with urushiol "poisoning" for a very, very long time. In 1987, *Archives in Dermatology* reported the find of a poison sumac leaf fossil in central Oregon deposits of volcanic ash. It was dated at 35 million years of age.

William T. Gillis, in a 1975 *Arnoldia* article, reported poison ivy fossils "from the western part of the United States from Oligocene time (40 million years ago)." He also noted that poison ivy no longer grows on the West Coast, which is now the province of poison oak, and that the poison ivy fossils "resemble more closely the poison-ivies of eastern Asia than they do extant poison-ivies from the country [United States] today."

The eastern Asian and North American poison ivies, said Gillis, probably "originated in North America about 80 million years ago and migrated across the Bering Straits when there was a land connection between North America and Asia, and when the climate was much milder." Upon the separation of the two continents, and changes in temperatures, different subspecies evolved on each continent.

Gillis described the first documentation of poison ivy in North America: seeds found in the medicine bag of a thirteenth-century southwestern U.S. American Indian. The first known North American written description was published by Captain John Smith in 1624. "An Anecdotal History of Poison Ivy," in *Archives in Dermatology*, 1955, reported other early writings published in 1635, the early 1700s, and 1751. But kudos for the literary origins of poison ivy belong to China. Gillis reported that "references to it are known in . . . writings of Chinese scholars back as far as the seventh century."

Even the scientific name for poison ivy's toxic oil harks from the Pacific Rim. "Urushiol," explained a 1945 article in the *Journal of the American Medical Association* (*JAMA*), derives from the Japanese word *kiurushi*, the sap of the Japanese lacquer tree.

East Asian interest in urushiol comes not so much from trouble with poison ivy, as from its *Toxicodendron* kin, which, said John H. Beaman, Ph.D., in "Asian Anacardiaceae," *Clinics in Dermatology*, 1986, thrives in eastern Asia. Of the approximately thirty *Toxicodendron* species worldwide, more than twenty are indigenous to eastern Asia. By comparison he identified only a handful in the western hemisphere, including the North American poison ivies, poison oaks, and poison sumac.

East Asian *Toxicodendron* grow mostly as trees. The Japanese or Chinese lacquer tree, *T. vernicifluum,* said Beaman, is a source of lacquer used for art in China "since before the beginning of the Christian era," and in Japan since the fourth century A.D.

T. succedaneae, he continued "is also used as a lacquer source in Indochina," while Japanese value the same tree more as a source of its urushiol-free wax, which is used in polishes and ointments.

In East Asia, continued Beaman, urushiol dermatitis is recognized as an industrial disease mostly "confined to workmen who gather the fresh sap or apply it." Reactions in the public at large usually come about from contact with furniture products treated with urushiol-laden lacquer. Contact with poison ivy seems not to be much of a problem. The East Asian countries have been highly populated for thousands of years. Land management over that time may have removed most of the wild growth.

Michigan poison ivy, 1961,
seed cluster

Mesa Verde poison ivy, about
1200, seed cluster

Comparison of poison ivy seed clusters. Those on the left are modern. The ones on the right were retrieved from cliff dwellings at Mesa Verde National Park, Colorado, and were radiocarbon-dated as having grown in the thirteenth century. *Arnoldia*. Volume 35, # 2. March/April 1975; reprinted with permission.

Because the dreaded dermatitis is caused by urushiol, no matter what continent it resides on or what plant or tree it courses through, persons sensitive to any flora containing the oil will be allergic to all flora containing it and even to products treated with *Toxicodendron* lacquer.

Sensitization to urushiol is also free-range in nature. As with all allergic reactions, a sensitizing encounter is usually necessary before a reaction can occur. The first time the body is exposed to urushiol, there is no allergic reaction. Instead the body is alerted to the existence of urushiol and classifies it as a dangerous substance. Only on subsequent exposures, depending on personal sensitivity, does the immune system leap into action. While

There was a very old book in our household (dating back to the nineteenth century) that contained many home remedies for various ailments. I believe that one dealing with poison ivy suggested that a mixture of cigar ashes and saliva would help control the itching. I never tried it—I preferred the itching!

—*G. D.*

reactions without a sensitizing encounter are possible, they are unusual—even rare.

A person previously sensitized to urushiol through contact with poison ivy can have an allergic reaction on first contact with *Toxicodendron* lacquer, such as that used on some furniture and (alas) toilet seats. And first-time visitors to North America who had gathered lacquer sap in China, or who leaned against a lacquered Chinese or Japanese credenza any place in the world, can react to poison ivy or oak even though they have never been in contact with it before.

> *. . . My severe case of the rash covered nearly all of my body. I was spread-eagled on a double bed and had nurses around the clock. I could not lift my terribly swollen arms to help myself and had to be fed through a tube, as my face and lips were badly swollen. . . .*
>
> *—E. M.*

In a manner consistent with its perverse nature, urushiol is not the only sensitizer to urushiol. The immune system, ever confused when it comes to allergies, can be sensitized to urushiol by contact with certain non-urushiol plants. Incidents of cross-reactivity have been clinically documented. An article in *Contact Dermatitis*, 1986, reports that sensitivity to the Australian plant "Robyn Gordon" can produce sensitivity to poison ivy. William Epstein, M.D., professor of dermatology, University of California, San Francisco, is participating in a study investigating apparent cross-reactivity between philodendrons and poison ivy.

Incidents of urushiol sensitivity and cross-reactivity are likely to increase as both plants and people make their way more easily around the world. South America, reported Ines Hurtado, M.D., Ph.D., in *Clinics in Dermatology*, 1986, has only a few native poisonous Anacardiaceae that have been identified to date, but is host to introduced species such as East Asian Anacardiaceae *T. succedaneum* and *T. vernicifluum* (lacquer or wax trees) and North American *T. radicans* (poison ivy) and *T. diversilobum* (poison oak).

The immigrant plants were probably brought to South America as ornamentals. John D. Mitchell, Ph.D., of the New York Botanical Garden, reported in conversation that Asian *T. succedaneum*, the Japanese wax tree, has escaped from cultivation in Brazil, where it now grows with the audacity of a weed.

Poison ivy has taken similar advantage of its import into England and Europe. As early as the 1600s, adventurers to the New World were taking specimens of this and other pretty plants back to their home countries. Epstein reports that poison ivy grows in Kew Gardens in England and has escaped from cultivation in the Scandinavian countries. Early in the twentieth century, he says, poison ivy was introduced to Holland as a stabilizer of the earth dikes that keep the sea at bay. From there it has escaped as well and is now working its way into the Black Forest in Germany.

This worldwide proliferation makes even more unlikely a dearly held fantasy of some urushiol sufferers: total eradication of the poison oaks and poison ivies. Poison sumac avoids the curse because it keeps so kindly to its isolated habitat. The oaks and ivies, however, like their component urushiol, spread, it seems, willy-nilly.

Both plants have two ways of getting around: roots and seeds. Their root systems are promiscuous. Runners expand a plant's domain by growing away from the parent plant and then sending up suckers that become parents in their own right.

Approximate worldwide native distribution of poison ivies and poison oaks. Poison oaks and poison ivies do not like rain forests or northern tundra. Hence they do not grow of their own initiative in Alaska, Hawaii, southern Mexico, South America, or Africa. (Adapted from map by William T. Gillis, *Arnoldia*, March-April 1975. Reprinted with permission.)

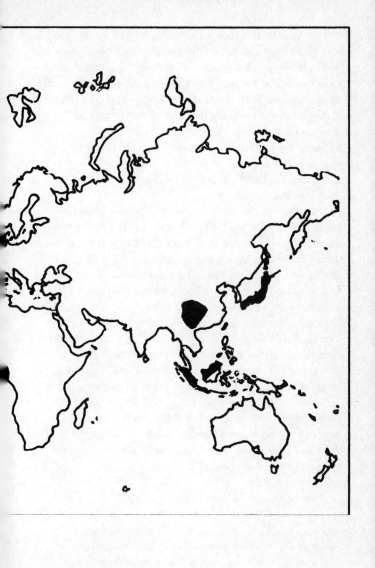

At least this method of reproduction keeps the poison ivy and oak patches in their original neighborhoods. Seeds, however, allow immigration. They are not so light as to be carried by wind, but birds are happy to take on the obligation. They lunch on the berries and, after they garner nourishment from the flesh of the fruit, expel the seeds as waste. Beds of poison ivy and oak are commonly found around utility poles and on the ground under their wires where birds tend to sit. They, and the animals that also partake of this treat, are the Johnny Appleseeds of the *Toxicodendron*.

The history and lore of attempts at poison ivy and oak eradication are, as befits the subjects, rife with desire and despair. An 1898 *Farmers' Bulletin* declared that "it is highly desirable that legal measures be adopted compelling the destruction of these plants where they abound in cities and in places of popular resort." The cry is repeated in 1908 in *Country Life in America*: "The poison ivy evil is serious enough to have the attention of city fathers and town selectmen. Certainly it is the office of highway commissioners to keep the roads safe and to use strong restrictive and preventive methods." The author, Frances Duncan, went on to recommend "a bounty given on ivy roots."

Prior to the development of our current herbicides, a variety of methods were used in eradication efforts. Grubbing out the roots was always an option. A 1910 article in the *Garden Magazine*, appealed to its readers to help rid their localities of the plight:

> Why not telephone two or three of your neighbors to come to your house some evening this week and figure out a plan for destroying all the poison ivy that lines the roadside from your respective homes to the railroad station? You may be immune, but think about the people who are blinded for a week and suffer all that time!

The author further suggested that "you can hire a gang of workmen to root it out with a pick, mattock and the hands."

Chemical treatments were also available. The favorites were as variable as early rash remedies. The one deemed most effective was treatment of the plants with sulphuric acid. The directions published in a 1920 *Farmers' Bulletin*

My earliest memory of the disease (1930s) is seeing school-mates with puffed up ghostly white calamine-lotioned hands and faces. And I remember vaguely, when I was quite young, the fate of Jenny, a young woman . . . when she strayed into the bushes in Gloucester and picked a huge bunch of shiny green poison ivy branches for a flower arrangement. Years later my mother said that Jenny nearly died.

My mother was also highly allergic to "the poise." I never got it until I was about fifteen. I got over (the first siege) only to get it again several weeks later. . . . Dr. Withington warned me against touching the blisters or coming in contact with water and prescribed a brown wash that my wife . . . thinks was called potassium permanganate. I had poison ivy all over, head to toe, blisters on top of blisters . . . and I painted myself with this horrible brown stuff and wandered around the house in shorts and bare feet. A friend of my mother's came to call one afternoon and screamed when I answered the door.

But somehow, even after strictly following Dr. Withington's orders and coating myself over and over with the brown stuff, I didn't seem to improve. In fact I seemed to get worse. Finally, desperate after a week or so of torture, I filled up the bathtub with cool water, plunged in, washed away the awful brown stuff, and at once felt fine! The poison ivy had apparently run its course, and the horrible brown wash was (now) causing the itching. . . .

—*F. P.*

are simple: "Apply a few drops . . . to the bases of the plants at intervals of a week until they die."

The same publication described the use of another popular agent, salt brine. Three pounds to a gallon of water could be sprayed on the plants to kill the leaves, although additional sprayings would be necessary to "kill the new shoots which soon arise from the rootstocks." When these methods did not work, the desperate turned to the barn for supplies: Kerosene or motor oil poured on the roots were sure to kill anything, if applied often enough and long enough.

Sadly, science has not taken us much further today. Contemporary herbicides do work, but sometimes they must be applied more than once; if the patch is very large, dreams of eradication will remain dreams. "It is not possible to eradicate poison ivy from acreage," said Clark Montgomery, Beltrami County extension agent, Bemidji, Minnesota. He does believe it is possible, however, to at least keep it at bay when it infringes on the personal space of your yard.

Folks who react only mildly to urushiol, are ecology minded, or are embarking on their first poison ivy or poison oak eradication adventure often seek nature-friendly methods. The first impulse is usually to grub out the roots. This works if the patch is not too large, but it must be done with diligence. Any root segments left in the ground are likely to sprout new plants.

Grubbers should also be forewarned that dermatologists report that the worst cases of urushiol reactions come from grubbing out roots, which are filled with urushiol. Every break in the system releases mega-amounts of the microquantities needed to cause a reaction. Urushiol can lie in wait on a shovel, a hoe, even on grass blades. Because of this, protective dress is essential. No bare legs, bare feet,

Root system for poison ivies and poison oaks. Because of high sap content, roots are rich in the oil urushiol, which causes poison ivy, oak, and sumac dermatitis. Illustration by Vivienne Morgan.

bare arms, bare hands. No wiping of sweat off the brow with a sleeve that may have also contacted a bit of root.

To maximize effectiveness of the rooting out, do it when the ground is soft and damp. The roots will yield more easily. To minimize paying for your good deed with two weeks of misery, do the grubbing in early spring or late fall when there are no leaves on the stems and sap is reduced. Still, be alert to the berries. They contain urushiol.

When you are done, and before you wash up, dispose of the remains of your kill. Whatever else you do, do not burn them. Urushiol is carried in smoke and can get into your eyes and lungs and onto your skin and clothes. And remember that the urushiol in the old roots and stems will still be active even years later. The only plant parts that do not contain the durable urushiol are the flowers and leaves that have died away and fallen from the plant as part of their natural cycle. Bag the leftovers and take them to a disposal site, remembering that the bottoms of the bags—if you set them down at the grub site—may carry urushiol that can be left in the trunk of your car. You can bag and bury, but check the interment site occasionally. Seeds hiding in the rubble can still find their way to light.

To protect yourself when you are done, throw away your gloves. The oil is surely well imbedded in the fabric or leather. With water sprayed from a hose, wash your boots and their bottoms well, as well as any tools you used. Remove your clothes outside, so you don't transfer urushiol to a kitchen chair, and wash them in copious amounts of water. Then wash yourself and your hair in copious amounts of water. Invisible droplets of urushiol may have flown through the air when you broke the roots and landed anywhere on you.

Then, as with any other method of eradication, keep an eye on the patch and, being appropriately paranoid about urushiol, immediately pull out any new plants that appear.

If you are more than mildly sensitive to urushiol, one episode of grubbing out, with its inevitable skin reaction, may prompt you to consider other methods of eradication. Covering the patch with a deep mulch or black plastic will work to a degree. The roots may make their way beyond the boundaries of your cover and send up new plants, but you can cover those too.

You could mow the patch again and again, but you'd be sorry: think of all those broken leaves and stems with

The tree [I played in] was [a cousin to] poison sumac. By morning the welts were everywhere there was to be found on my face and hands. Mounds were swelling and blistering like boiling vats of flesh. The shape of my face disappeared, overtaken by the growing mass. Involuntarily I held my fingers spread wide apart as the bubbles grew out of the patches of skin between them. Mother and Fukudasan covered me with calamine lotion. I lay in it as though embalmed, rigid and still. Someone brought in an electric fan and put it in the chair beside my face. I turned to face the breeze it made. The wind against the initial wetness of the chalky lotion brought almost total relief for a few minutes. Then the heat generated from inside set about its boiling and itching and baking until the . . . white film of lotion baked and flaked and turned useless. I was in a mild trance, willing the itch away. I reverted to scratching when my will power broke down. Wherever I scratched got worse. Wherever I touched got infected—new welts roiled up to the surface within hours. My brain was numbed. I lay focused on quelling the rising itch and the urge to scratch.

I crossed the room and looked into the mirror above the dresser. I saw a mask, a pitiful mask made of wounded flesh on wounded flesh. My eyes were holes, barely visible behind cursory cut-outs left in the distended skin. What had been my nose was a monstrous bulbous ball made of a foreign substance which could have been painted papier-mâché as well anything else. My cheeks were puffed and craggy mountains. At that moment terror overwhelmed my numbness and my faithful meditation. . . . Tears squeezed out of sunken eyes and down their salty rivulets through the mud flats of calamine lotion. . . . It didn't cross my mind to ask if my face would come back. I knew it was gone forever. . . .

—*From a memoir by Meggan Moorhead about growing up in Japan, 1950–1968* urushiol gushing out onto your legs and shoes and yard. Or you could even try the early brine solution, but not the kerosene or motor oil. It is now illegal to pour such products into the earth.

Or you could turn to corporate-style chemistry. There are two kinds of poisons that will work: those that kill everything green and those that kill only green things with broad leaves, as opposed to grasses. The University of Minnesota Extension Service recommends any herbicide with triclopyr, a woody brush killer that is effective on poison oak and poison ivy.

The best way to choose a commercial poison is to consult with nurseries or agriculture services in your area. In most states poison ivy and oak are registered Noxious Weeds. In Minnesota that means they are "deemed by the Commissioner of Agriculture to be injurious to public health, public roads . . . and other property. . . ."

Whatever poison you choose, follow the directions carefully so that you can protect yourself and your land while accomplishing the only reasonable goal—a truce. As with grubbing out, no matter which chemical you use, you will have to monitor the site and be prepared to continue treatment. And be alert, too, for sprouts in new places. The farmer birds are always at work.

Bibliography

The American Educator: A Library of University Knowledge. Philadelphia: Syndicate Publishing Company, 1897, 2562.

Beaman, John, Ph.D. "Allergenic Asian Anacardiaceae." *Clinics in Dermatology* 4, no. 2 (April–June 1986): 191–203.

Chesnut, V. K. *Thirty Poisonous Plants: Farmers' Bulletin no. 86.* Washington, D.C.: Government Printing Office, U.S. Department of Agriculture, 1898.

"The Contributors Club: *Rhus Toxicodendron.*" *The Atlantic Monthly* (June 1923): 858–59.

The Doo-Wop Songbook. New York: The Goodman Group, 1989.

Duncan, Frances. "Poison Ivy and Its Eradication." *Country Life in America* XIV, no. 5 (September 1908): 482.

Epstein, William L., M.D. "Occupational Poison Ivy and Oak Dermatitis." *Dermatologic Clinics* 4, no. 2 (April–June 1986): 511–16.

—— and V. S. Byers, Ph.D. *Poison Oak and Poison Ivy Dermatitis—Prevention and Treatment in Forest Service Work.* Missoula, MT 59801, USDA Forest Service Equipment Development Center, Publication 8167 2803 (1981).

Foster, Steven, et al. *A Field Guide to Medicinal Plants: Eastern and Central North America, Peterson Field Guide Series.* New York: Houghton Mifflin, 1990.

Frankel, Edward, Ph.D. *Poison Ivy, Poison Oak, Poison Sumac and Their Relatives.* Pacific Grove, California: Boxwood, 1991.

Gibbons, Euell. *Stalking the Wild Asparagus.* New York: David McKay Company, 1962.

Gillis, William T. "Poison-Ivy and Its Kin." *Arnoldia* 35, no. 2 (March/April 1975), 93–121.

———. "The Systematics and Ecology of Poison Ivy and the Poison Oaks." *Rhodora* 73, no. 793 (1971): 72–161.

Goldman, Leon, M.D. "The Antiquity of Poison Sumac" (letter). *Archives of Dermatology* 123 (January 1987): 27.

Goodman, Herman. "Ivy Poisoning: How to Escape It and Why." *Hygeia: The Health Magazine* 8 (August 1927): 384–85.

Grant, C. V, and A. A. Hansen. "Poison Ivy and Poison Sumac and Their Eradication." *Farmers' Bulletin 1166*, U.S. Department of Agriculture, Washington, D.C. (1920).

Guin, Jere D., M.D., and John H. Beaman, Ph.D. "Toxico-dendrons of the United States." *Clinics in Dermatology*, vol. 4, no. 2 (April–June 1986): 137–48.

Hurtado, Ines, M.D., Ph.D. "Poisonous Anacardiaceae of South America." *Clinics in Dermatology* 4, no. 2 (April–June 1986): 183–90.

"Iron-Treatment for Poison Ivy." *The Literary Digest* XC, no. 4 (July 24, 1926): 22–23.

"Ivy Poisoning: How to Treat It." *The Literary Digest* LXXXI, no. 6 (May 10, 1924): 23.

Jessup, Elon. "The Poison Squad of the Woods." *Outing* 81 (January 1923): 161–63.

Mansfield, Charles Monroe, M.D. "Three Poisonous Plants." *Country Life America* XXII, no. 4 (June 15, 1912): 39–40.

Marks, James G. Jr., M.D., J. F. Fowler Jr., M.D., Elizabeth F. Sherertz, M.D., and Robert L. Rietschel, M.D. "Prevention of Poison Ivy and Poison Oak Allergic Contact Dermatitis by Quarternium-18 Bentonite." *Journal of the American Academy of Dermatology* 33, no. 2, part 1 (August 1995): 212–16.

Masenbarb, John. *Poison Ivy and Its Control.* St. Paul: Minnesota Extension Service, University of Minnesota, 1991.

McAdam, Thomas. "Roadside Gardening: Exterminate Poison Ivy." *The Garden Magazine* (June 1910): 328.

McDonnell, Evelyn. "Stay Sick." *Rolling Stone* (May 3, 1990): 89.

Menz, Jennifer, et al. "Contact Dermatitis from *Grevillea* 'Robyn Gordon.'" *Contact Dermatitis* 15 (1986): 126–31.

Mitchell, John, D., Ph.D. "The Poisonous Anacardiaceae Genera of the World." *Advances in Economic Botany*, New York Botanical Garden 8 (1990): 103–23.

The New Century Dictionary of the English Language, New York: D. Appleton-Century Company, 1927, 1347.

Noxious Weeds. Undated pamphlet, circa 1980s. St. Paul: Minnesota Department of Agriculture, Agronomy Division.

Ornstein, Robert, Ph.D., and Sobel, David. *The Healing Brain.* New York: Simon & Schuster, 1987.

"Poison Ivy Conquered by Simple Chemicals." *Scientific American* (August 1927): 162–63.

"Poison Ivy's Large Clan." *The Literary Digest* XC (August 1925): 60–61.

Rice, William S. "Suspicious Characters of the Woods." *Outing* 40 (August 1902): 551–54

Rostenberg, Adolph Jr., M.D. "An Anecdotal Biographical History of Poison Ivy." *AMA Archives of Dermatology* 72 (1955): 438–45.

Smith, John, Capt. *The Generall Historie of Virginia, New-England, and the Summer Isles . . .* II. Reprinted 1986,

Philip L. Barbour, Ed. Chapel Hill: University of North Carolina Press, 1642.

Spencer, Edwin Rollin. *All About Weeds.* New York: Dover Publications, Inc., 1974.

Stevens, Franklin, M.D. "Status of Poison Ivy Extracts." *Journal of the American Medical Association* (April 7, 1945): 912–21.

"Turning a Leaf." *Time* (May 28, 1984): 89.

Watson, E. Sue. "*Toxicodendron* Hyposensitization Programs." *Clinics in Dermatology,* 4, no. 2 (April–June 1986): 160–70.

Zink, B. J., et al. "The Effect of Jewel Weed in Preventing Poison Ivy Dermatitis." *Journal of Wilderness Medicine* 2 (1991): 178–82.

Index

About the Author

Susan Carol Hauser is a former commentator on National Public Radio and teaches writing at Bemidji State University in northern Minnesota. She is the award-winning author of numerous books including *A Field Guide to Ticks: Prevent and Treat Lyme Disease and Other Ailments Caused by Ticks, Scorpions, Spiders, and Mites*; *Wild Rice Cooking: History, Natural History, Harvesting and Lore*; and *Sugaring: A Maple Syrup Memoir with Instructions*.

Other books by Hauser include:

Nonfiction
You Can Write a Memoir
Full Moon: Reflections on Turning Fifty
Girl to Woman: A Gathering of Images
Which Way to Look
Meant to Be Read Out Loud
What the Animals Know

Poetry
Outside after Dark: New & Selected Poems
Redpoll on a Broken Branch